£6.95

KU-198-097

Crime and Disorder

ISSUES

Volume 7

Editor

Craig Donnellan

Independence

Educational Publishers
Cambridge

30130504308960

First published by Independence
PO Box 295
Cambridge CB1 3XP
England

British Library Cataloguing in Publication Data
Crime and Disorder – (Issues Series)
I. Donnellan, Craig II. Series
364

ISBN 1 86168 203 4

Printed in Great Britain
The Burlington Press
Cambridge

Typeset by
Claire Boyd

Cover
The illustration on the front cover is by
Pumpkin House.

CONTENTS

OOO668 141 9 OO10

Introduction

Crime and Disorder is the seventh volume in the Issues series. The aim of this series is to offer up-to-date information about important issues in our world.

Crime and Disorder examines the trends in crime, young offenders and crime prevention.

The information comes from a wide variety of sources and includes:
Government reports and statistics
Newspaper reports and features
Magazine articles and surveys
Literature from lobby groups
and charitable organisations.

It is hoped that, as you read about the many aspects of the issues explored in this book, you will critically evaluate the information presented. It is important that you decide whether you are being presented with facts or opinions. Does the writer give a biased or an unbiased report? If an opinion is being expressed, do you agree with the writer?

Crime and Disorder offers a useful starting-point for those who need convenient access to information about the many issues involved. However, it is only a starting-point. At the back of the book is a list of organisations which you may want to contact for further information.

*****

Britain leads the world on risk of being assaulted

By Philip Johnston, Home Affairs Editor

Violent crime is rising faster in England and Wales than anywhere else in Europe, new figures showed yesterday.

In 1999, robberies and assaults rose by 16 per cent compared with five per cent across the rest of the EU. Overall levels of violence were far higher in Britain than in countries of comparable size.

There were 703,000 assaults recorded by police in 1999 – more than twice the number only four years earlier. This compared with 186,000 in Germany and 216,000 in France. The risk of assault, while low, is higher in Britain than almost anywhere else in the industrialised world, including America. Only in Australia is it greater.

International crime comparisons released by the Home Office showed that the British also faced a far greater risk of being burgled despite recent falls in property crime. Between 1995 and 1999, break-ins dropped by 30 per cent but still remained above 400,000. In France, by contrast, there were 191,000 burglaries and in Germany, a country of 82 million people, there were 142,000.

Ominously, the rate of decrease is slowing in Britain. Between 1998 and 1999, there was a six per cent fall in burglaries while France registered an eight per cent fall and Germany 11 per cent. The chances of having a car stolen were also higher in Britain than almost anywhere in Europe.

On the eve of an election in which law and order will feature prominently, ministers have been anxious to claim that crime is falling. Charles Clarke, Home Office minister, said that, between 1995 and 1999, overall levels of recorded crime fell faster in England and Wales than the EU average.

However, most of this decline took place under the Tories. Between 1997 and 1999, the total number of recorded crimes went up by almost 800,000 at a time when numbers in France and Germany were virtually stable and in America were falling dramatically.

Mr Clarke said the Government relied more on the British Crime

> **Between 1997 and 1999, the total number of recorded crimes went up by almost 800,000 at a time when numbers in France and Germany were virtually stable**

Survey as 'a more accurate reflection of crime levels and trends'. He said it showed a greater decline than that shown in the recorded crime figures, especially where violent crime was concerned.

Mr Clarke said: 'There is little doubt that the recorded figures demonstrate a much greater willingness of victims to report crimes of violence, and for the police to record them. Comparing the recorded crime statistics of different countries is also always difficult because of a wide variation in recording practices, counting rules and offence definitions.'

But whatever gloss the Government tried to place on the statistics, they showed Britain to be one of the most crime-ridden countries in the industrialised world. The report's authors said: 'Of the 17 countries examined, England and Wales had well above average levels of property and contact crime – i.e. robbery, assault and sexual assault.'

High crime levels in Britain also mean that rates of imprisonment are greater than elsewhere in the EU. In England and Wales, the rate is 125 per 100,000 population and in Scotland 118. Only Portugal has a higher rate in the EU.

While penal reformers criticise the high levels of imprisonment in Britain, the level of crime means the use of custody per offence is no greater than the EU average. The highest levels of imprisonment are found in Russia, the United States and South Africa. The lowest among industrialised nations is Japan but this is because it has the least crime.

The one crumb of comfort from the figures is that homicide rates are lower in Britain than elsewhere. In England and Wales, the rate is 1.45 per 100,000 compared with 1.63 in France, 1.28 in Germany and 2.60 in Spain.

The highest murder rates are in South Africa, where there were 23,800 homicides in 1999 at a rate of 56.49; Russia with nearly 30,000 (20.5); and America, where there have been dramatic falls in crime, with 15,000 homicides at a rate of 6.26 per 100,000 population.

London has one of the lowest homicide rates among the world's major cities. The least safe included in the Home Office survey were Washington DC, Pretoria, Moscow and Tallinn in Estonia.

Violence rules: not OK

By Andrew Alderson and Jenny Booth

An estate agent is stabbed in the face; two gangs shoot it out in a restaurant; a jury hears of a 10-year-old boy brutally murdered on the street: just another wet Wednesday in Britain. As Andrew Alderson and Jenny Booth report, violent crime has risen dramatically over the past two decades – but the most worrying news is that the trend is accelerating rapidly

It was just before 4pm last Wednesday when Tim Robinson, a genial, athletic, 25-year-old estate agent, died. He had been in intensive care for three days after being stabbed in the face, chest and arm by two youths as he parked his Audi 3 Quattro outside his home in Battersea, south London.

At the same time on Wednesday, five miles from St Thomas's, the hospital where Mr Robinson died, an argument developed in a busy Nando's restaurant in Shepherd's Bush during which youths pulled out handguns and began firing. The group fled, leaving a 28-year-old waitress bleeding from a wound to her arm.

A 17-year-old youth seriously wounded in the gun battle struggled to his nearby car but, shortly after driving off, he struck a moped rider, collided with another car and ploughed through a shop window. The driver died at the wheel but no one inside the shop was injured.

Also at the same time, on the same day, two miles in the other direction from St Thomas's hospital, an Old Bailey jury was nearing the end of its first day of evidence hearing allegations that Damilola Taylor, 10, was stabbed to death 'for a laugh' by four teenagers.

A broken bottle had been pushed into his leg and twisted so the wound would stay open and a marble had been stuffed down his throat to stifle his screams, the court was told.

Just an hour in the capital on a blustery Wednesday afternoon had seen a catalogue of carnage unfold. For Britain in the year 2002 is a nation in which the number of violent crimes and the level of force used are rising dramatically.

Certainly, London witnessed two firsts it could have done without last Wednesday: Britain's first suspected 'carjack' killing and the first fatal daylight gun battle fought by rival gangs in a restaurant.

It was also the day on which many newspapers led their front pages with headlines announcing a supposed new initiative from Lord

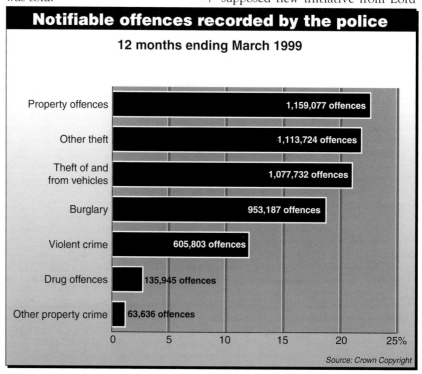

Notifiable offences recorded by the police

12 months ending March 1999

- Property offences — 1,159,077 offences
- Other theft — 1,113,724 offences
- Theft of and from vehicles — 1,077,732 offences
- Burglary — 953,187 offences
- Violent crime — 605,803 offences
- Drug offences — 135,945 offences
- Other property crime — 63,636 offences

0   5   10   15   20   25%

Source: Crown Copyright

Woolf, the Lord Chief Justice, to tackle a surge in street muggings. Under revised guidelines, the stories read, mobile phone muggers should be jailed for at least 18 months even if they are young, unarmed, first offenders.

Those who use weapons or violence should expect sentences of five years or more. However, the Lord Chief Justice, in fact, was just confirming the existing punishment tariffs for these offences.

Violent crime has been rising for decades. It dropped significantly after the Second World War, but in recent decades offences have crept up relentlessly.

In the past 20 years, the number of crimes of violence against the person – everything from common assault to murder – recorded by the police in England and Wales has increased more than 2.5 times; from 100,200 in 1981 to 276,000 in 2001.

The use of guns and knives is also on the increase. In England and Wales, handguns were used in 3,685 crimes in 2000 compared with 2,648 in 1997: an increase of 40 per cent, despite the fact that handgun ownership was banned in 1997, proving the argument made at the time that the ban would affect only the law-abiding and not the criminals.

The use of violence appears to be accelerating. Statistics from the Metropolitan Police show a 50 per cent increase in muggings in the last three months of 2001 compared with the previous year. There are now more than 4,500 reports of robbery each month.

The police, criminologists and sociologists offer various explanations for the growth in violent crime: poor discipline at home and at school; greater upheaval in society leaving more disaffected people; wider availability of alcohol and drugs, and the greater number of valuables to steal in our affluent society have all been blamed for the trend.

Michael Levi, professor of criminology at Cardiff University, says, however, that levels of thuggery have some way to go before they match the violence of Victorian times.

In the second half of the 19th

century the rate of assaults against the police – seen as a useful measure of violent lawlessness in society – was higher than now.

While acknowledging there was heavy drinking in Victorian times, he said: 'Today there are more people crazed on drugs and alcohol or a combination of the two. I can understand people feeling that there is more meaningless violence around.'

Other criminologists and the police say the degree of violence used – the willingness of criminals to be brutal and cruel for no reason – is also worsening.

'Today there are more people crazed on drugs and alcohol or a combination of the two. I can understand people feeling that there is more meaningless violence around'

Senior police officers are appalled by the recent level of violent crime. Det. Supt Trevor Shepherd, who is leading the hunt for the killers of Mr Robinson, who was stabbed in front of his girlfriend, described the assault as savage.

'He didn't really stand a chance. This was a vicious and violent and totally unprovoked attack,' he said.

Det. Chief Insp. Duncan Wilson, who works with the Operation

Trident focus on black-on-black crime and who is investigating the Sherpherd's Bush shooting, said: 'The illegal handgun is seen as an essential item for peer respect by so many today. The sad thing is that they are also prepared to use them indiscriminately for such petty reasons.'

The Metropolitan Police insists that it is doing all it can to tackle violent crime: last month it announced that it was transferring an extra 500 officers to target street crime.

Michael Todd, the assistant commissioner at Scotland Yard, said he believed the increase in violent crime was partly linked to drug use, with turf wars over supplying drugs and people committing crimes to 'feed' their habits. 'An individual is not that likely to be the victim of crime, but if people feel imprisoned in their home that deeply worries me,' he said.

It is not just London that is witnessing a rise in vicious and unprovoked crimes. On Thursday, a court heard how Claire Robson, 21, the daughter of the former England soccer captain Bryan Robson, had been violently attacked as she tried to book a taxi home after a night out in Durham.

Her 'offence' was to have been recognised as the daughter of the former manager of Middlesbrough by a drunken 20-year-old who hurled abuse at her before headbutting her so hard that she suffered a gash to her face that required 10 stitches.

If the experiences of other victims of crime are anything to go by, Miss Robson may take years to recover from her ordeal.

Lesley Clarke, the wife and business partner of Nicky, the celebrated hairdresser, is frightened to go out alone after she was mugged outside her home in St John's Wood, north London, two years ago.

She was forced to the ground and one man held his hands over her mouth as another ripped off her jewellery, cutting her fingers as he took her rings.

The nature of violent crime has changed over time. Bank and post office robberies have almost stopped because new technology has made such crimes harder to commit.

In their place has come the trend toward street muggings for mobile phones. Police records show that 330,000 mobiles were stolen in 2000-01, but estimates based on the *British Crime Survey* and two studies of theft among school pupils suggest the true figure may be closer to 710,000.

The most recent crime phenomenon is carjacking. The Metropolitan Police has recorded 100 incidents of the violent theft of cars from owners in the past year.

Police believe that sophisticated security systems on modern cars have led thieves to resort to stealing vehicles directly from their owners in the street, or following them home to rob them of their keys. Extreme violence is very much part of the modus operandi of the carjacker.

Opinions are divided on how to tackle the violence. Although Lord Woolf's initiative against mobile phone thefts has been welcomed by the public, tough words in the past have not been met by tough action. Longer sentences have not always led to reduced crime.

Under Jack Straw's so-called 'three strikes and you're out' law, the Crime Sentences Act 1997 ruled that third-time burglars should serve a minimum of three years.

A year after the Act came into force in 1999, however, it was found that judges had shunned their new powers and not a single burglar had been sentenced under its provisions. Plans for a 'three strikes' rule for mobile phone thieves were raised by ministers a month ago, but the idea appears to have been dropped.

Prof. Levi, the criminologist, said that when there was a surge of public fear of muggings in the 1980s – and sentences for muggings became heavier – the effect on the level of offending was minimal.

'I don't actually think that kids [who are planning to steal a mobile] are likely to be turning their minds that much to sentencing,' he said. 'Heavier sentences will have some effect, but I wouldn't put my money on a dramatic drop in mobile telephone crime.'

Fred Broughton, the president of the Police Federation, the union for rank-and-file officers in England and Wales, blames the Government for allowing police numbers to fall in the late 1990s, hampering the campaign against violent crime.

'The police service must dramatically increase in size to enable police officers to take back the streets and combat violent crime,' he said. The Conservative Party claims Labour is soft on violent criminals.

Oliver Letwin, the Shadow Home Secretary, says: 'Labour promised to be tough on crime, but violent crime has soared since they came to power. Once again, they have failed to live up to their rhetoric.'

The police insist that the public must not carry illegal weapons such as guns and knives to defend themselves. Instead, they advise people to keep to well-lit areas at night, to keep valuables hidden and, if confronted, not to resist or tackle their assailants but hand over whatever it is the criminal wants.

Car drivers are advised to keep their distance from other drivers, to lock their doors in traffic or if bumped from behind, and to hand over their keys if threatened.

Yet, as Tim Robinson discovered last week, in Britain in 2002 it is possible to follow all the rules – and still lose your life while parking your car outside your home.

© *Telegraph Group Limited, London 2002*

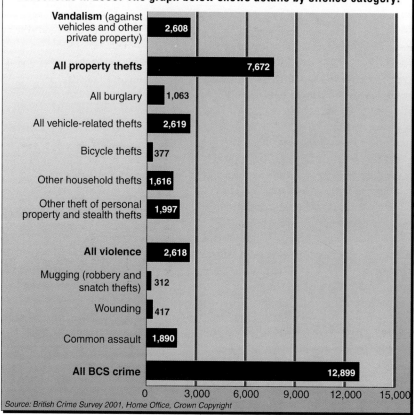

Extent of crime in 2000

The *British Crime Survey* (BCS) measures crime against adults (16 and over) living in private households in England and Wales. It has been conducted by the Home Office nine times since 1982. This is the first report from the 2001 sweep, which measured crime occurring in 2000. The BCS estimates there were 12,899 crimes against adults living in private households in 2000. The graph below shows details by offence category.

Offence category	Number
Vandalism (against vehicles and other private property)	2,608
All property thefts	7,672
All burglary	1,063
All vehicle-related thefts	2,619
Bicycle thefts	377
Other household thefts	1,616
Other theft of personal property and stealth thefts	1,997
All violence	2,618
Mugging (robbery and snatch thefts)	312
Wounding	417
Common assault	1,890
All BCS crime	12,899

Source: British Crime Survey 2001, Home Office, Crown Copyright

Chance of being a crime victim 'at 20-year low'

Crime is not as bad as people think it is, David Blunkett said yesterday. Despite a recent spate of street robberies and a huge increase in mobile telephone thefts, the Home Secretary said the chances of becoming a victim were at their lowest for 20 years.

'Anyone reading recent reports would think that crime and violent crime in particular is now spiralling out of control,' he said.

'The reality is very different. There is a growing problem with street robbery and mobile phones in particular. But overall crime is now falling and has been for some time.'

His speech in Sheffield marked a riposte to this week's attempts by Oliver Letwin, the shadow home secretary, to recapture the law and order agenda for the Conservatives.

He urged the creation of a 'neighbourly society' and acknowledged that society had a role in shaping criminal behaviour.

Mr Blunkett – who plans to visit New York in the spring to find out how the city has brought about reductions in crime – also emphasised the importance of 'building stronger communities that are empowered to take responsibility themselves for making the places where they live and work safer'.

He added: 'We all carry responsibility for the society and communities in which we live. The Government takes its responsibilities seriously to prevent and reduce crime and to build stronger communities. But others have to do the same.

'That means everyone from Government to police and the wider criminal justice system, family, individuals and the wider community.

'All of us have responsibility for the society we live in. I accept mine on behalf of the Government, but nobody else should be passing the buck either. Only by combined endeavour can we change the communities in which we live.'

*By Philip Johnston,
Home Affairs Editor*

He maintained that the Government was delivering its promises and had presided over large falls in burglaries and car thefts, although this trend began before Labour took office.

> *'Crime is falling overall, the chance of becoming a victim of crime is at its lowest for 20 years and we will shortly have a record number of police officers'*

'Crime is falling overall, the chance of becoming a victim of crime is at its lowest for 20 years and we will shortly have a record number of police officers,' Mr Blunkett said.

'But the key challenge remains to reduce not only the level of crime itself, but also the fear of crime felt by individuals and communities.'

Mr Blunkett runs the risk of sounding complacent at a time when violent crime continues to rise. He acknowledged the high levels of public concern over the rates of street robbery but believed that this could be tackled.

'Five years ago public concern was highest over the high volume crimes of burglary and vehicle crime that affect the most people,' he said.

'Now, thanks to a huge push by Government and all concerned, the rates for those offences have dropped significantly.

'I want to give credit to car manufacturers for playing their part in making their products harder to steal and I am now looking for the mobile phone industry to do the same.'

While Mr Blunkett is right to point out that burglaries have fallen and that the trend appears to be down, the number of domestic break-ins remains at a historically high level.

Youth crime

Some facts about young people who offend – 2000

Introduction

The following information is based largely upon information derived from Home Office *Criminal Statistics for England and Wales*, the most recent volume of which provides data relating to 2000. It attempts to provide an overview of trends within youth crime suggested by official statistics and to place that factual information in a broader context. The main focus is young people aged 10-17 years but some information on young adults, up to the age of 21 years, is included.

Two points should be noted about the figures for this year. First, they cover the period during which the major part of the reforms of the youth justice system were introduced. However, the measures were rolled out, following piloting, part-way through the 12 months. As a consequence the statistics combine information from before and after implementation and it is therefore difficult to assess any impact of those reforms upon the data.

Second, this is likely to be the last year that *Criminal Statistics* are presented in their current form. In future, official data from which the statistics are derived will be presented alongside results of the *British Crime Survey* (which is itself to be extended from a sample of 20,000 to 40,000) in a new annual *Picture of Crime*.

The extent of youth crime

Offending by young people is relatively common. A recent self-report survey administered to school children in 2001, for example, found that 43.9% of boys and 37.4% of girls in year 11 admitted having stolen items in the past. At the same time, contrary to public perception, the majority of crime is not attributable to young people. Thus during 2000, 88% of detected crime was, in fact, committed by persons over the age of 18. Moreover, adult offenders over the age of 21 were responsible for 81% of such offending. (By comparison, 10% of males have a criminal conviction by the age of 18 and around 30% by the age of 30.)

Furthermore, again contrary to popular perceptions, youth offending appears to have been falling for some years. The numbers of young people cautioned or sentenced for indictable offences show a gradual, through not uninterrupted, decline over the recent past and the latest figures show a continuation of that trend. Between 1992 and 2000, 10-17-year-olds convicted or cautioned for an indictable offence fell from 143,400 to 113,600: a decline of almost 21%. The pattern for those under 21-years is similar, though slightly less marked, falling from 240,600 in 1992 to 196,200 in 2000: a reduction of some 18%.

Moreover, youth crime has also fallen when expressed as a proportion of the youth population. Thus the number of young people cautioned or convicted of an indictable offence, per 100,000 population in the relevant age group, fell for 10-17-year-olds from 2,673 in 1992 to 1,947 in 2000. The equivalent figures for 18-20-year-olds are 4,632 and 4,177.

The fact that the trend for the under-18 age group has persisted beyond 1998 might be thought particularly significant. The introduction of the reprimand and final warning scheme (and anticipation of its introduction after the passing of the Crime and Disorder Act) is likely to have led to a reduction in the practice, previously fairly common in many police service areas, of dealing with first-time minor offending through an informal warning. Such informal disposals were not included in the figures for cautions. In the event, therefore, that offending which would not previously have been reflected in the statistics is now recorded as a reprimand or final warning, a rise in the figures might have been anticipated.

It might be argued that recorded youth crime does give a true reflection of overall patterns of youth offending. It is, for example, true that only around 50% of offences are reported to the police and, in addition, because of differences in recording practices between police service areas, not all reported offences appear as recorded crimes. Moreover, until an offence is 'cleared up', the age of the person committing it cannot be ascertained and a relatively small proportion of recorded crime is detected.

It is encouraging, therefore, that the decline in recorded and detected offending is matched by reductions in victimisation as measured through self-report studies by the *British Crime Survey*. The 2001 survey shows that, between 1995 and 2000, crime fell by 33%, averaging around 6% a year. In addition, there were reductions in offending between 1999 and 2000 in nearly all categories of offences measured by the survey: burglary by 17%, vehicle-related theft by 11% and violent crime by 19%. (A decrease indicated for robbery over the same twelve-month period, of 22%, is not however statistically significant due to the relatively low numbers of cases on which the figure is based.)

While victimisation gives a picture of overall crime rather than just that committed by young people, the pattern displayed by victim reports might be thought to add weight to the suggestion that the decline in recorded youth crime may represent a real phenomenon.

It should be noted for the

purposes of future comparison, that the Home Office is attempting to engender greater consistency in the recording procedures adopted by the police. Currently some areas only record offences where the police consider that there is sufficient evidence to prosecute, known as evidential recording. By contrast, other areas adopt what is known as prima facie recording, according to which recording of an offence depends on what is reported to the police by the public. The Association of Chief Police Officers has now produced guidance which promotes recording 'towards the prima facie end of the spectrum'. In these circumstances, it is likely that the new procedures will generate a large increase in recorded crime. Such an increase would not, however, necessarily reflect any change in the actual level of offending.

The nature of youth offending

The great majority of offences committed by young people are directed against property. Thus in 2000, theft, handling stolen goods, burglary, fraud or forgery and criminal damage, accounted for more than 68% of youth crime. Indeed theft and handling stolen goods alone, generally regarded as less serious property offences, account for more than 50% of crimes committed by those under the age of 18.

Despite the high media attention accorded to violent offending, just under 13% of cautions or convictions relate to violence against the person. While this does represent a small increase in the percentage of offending over the previous year, the actual number of violent offences has fallen steadily from 16,000 in 1993, 14,800 in 1996 to 14,600 in 2000. Perhaps more tellingly, 57% of such offences, in the latter year, resulted in a caution, suggesting that they arose out of incidents of a less serious nature. Similarly, robbery – another high profile offence – continues to be rare, accounting for 2.4% of all indictable offences. Again, the number of robberies committed by young people has declined slightly since 1996 from 3,000 to 2,700 although over the longer period there has been a rise:

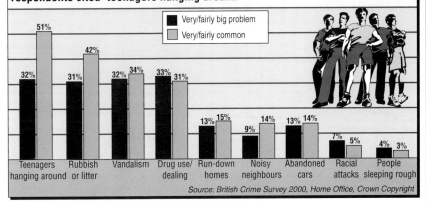

Levels of disorder in the 2000 BCS

Nationally, drug use or dealing, vandalism, teenagers hanging around on the streets and litter were considered to be the biggest local problems. When asked which particular type of disorder was most common in the local area, a third of respondents cited 'teenagers hanging around'

Legend: Very/fairly big problem · Very/fairly common

Teenagers hanging around 32% / 51%; Rubbish or litter 31% / 42%; Vandalism 32% / 34%; Drug use/dealing 33% / 31%; Run-down homes 13% / 15%; Noisy neighbours 9% / 14%; Abandoned cars 13% / 14%; Racial attacks 7% / 5%; People sleeping rough 4% / 3%

Source: British Crime Survey 2000, Home Office, Crown Copyright

from 2,100 in 1993. A recent research study by the Home Office suggests that a significant proportion of that increase is accounted for by theft of mobile phones, 48% of which involve victims under the age of 18.

The pattern of offending by young adults aged 18-20 displays a similar picture with violence against the person and robberies accounting for 11.3% and 2.4% respectively of offending leading to caution or conviction. Drugs offences are, however, much more prevalent amongst this age group and constitute just over 25% of the total.

The characteristics of young people who offend

An increasing amount is known about the risk factors which may be associated with offending behaviour among young people and recent research is usefully summarised in a report prepared by Communities that Care for the Youth Justice Board. Drawing on data derived from a national survey and a number of collated local surveys, the report estimates the prevalence of risk for a range of factors thought to be linked to youth offending. The results suggest that such risk factors apply to very large numbers of children and young people. Thus more than one-fifth of the sampled population, aged 10-16, fall into the group assessed to be most at risk for the following factors: family conflict, parents condoning problem behaviour, peers condoning problem behaviour, alienation and lack of social commitment, family history of problem

behaviour, low school achievement and aggressive behaviour including bullying.

In addition to establishing prevalence, however, the report also assesses the 'salience' of the same range of factors to youth crime and anti-social behaviour: that is, it measures the extent to which high risk in relation to a particular factor increases the odds of exclusion from school, being arrested and self reported offending. Poor school achievement, lack of commitment to school, family history of problem behaviour, peer involvement in behaviour and availability of drugs all score particularly highly on each of these three dimensions. The association of drugs misuse and offending is also confirmed by the *Youth Lifestyles Survey*. Serious or persistent offenders were much more likely to report using cannabis or heroin within the last twelve months (56% and 13% respectively) than those who reported never committing an offence (13% and 1%).

In terms of recorded crime, most children and young people who offend, almost 80%, are male. In 2000, 22.6% of young people convicted or cautioned for indictable offences were girls. Furthermore this proportion appears to have been relatively constant since, at least, the early 1990s. In each of the ten years between 1991 and 2000, the representation of girls within the youth offending population stayed within a range of 20.3% to 23.5%. Recent suggestions, within the media, that girls are increasingly likely to become involved in criminal activity do not therefore appear to be borne out by the data for recorded crime.

Furthermore, girls' offending is significantly less likely than that of their male counterparts to consist in serious offences such as violence against the person or robbery which account for 7.3% and 1.2% of female youth cautions and convictions.

The overrepresentation of black young people within the youth justice system, at almost every level, continues to be a cause of concern. While latest estimates put the proportion of the population in England and Wales of black ethnic origin at 2%, black or black British young people account for 6.1% of the population sentenced through the youth justice system. More worryingly, the overrepresentation is particularly marked at the level of custody with 8.5% of those subject to a detention and training order and 21.8% of those sentenced to long-term detention under section 91, recorded as black or black British. There is, however, no statistical difference in patterns of self-reported offending by black and white young people.

Conclusion

The most recent *Criminal Statistics* give a picture of the youth justice system at a point where major reform was implemented. To a large degree, they suggest a continuation of previously identified trends: in particular, a continued reduction in detected youth crime and an increase in the rate of prosecution. In relation to custody, the picture is slightly more complicated. While the rate of detention increased slightly, the absolute numbers of young people subject to custodial orders may finally have reached a plateau after a decade of rapid escalation.

• All statistical information in this article comes from *Criminal Statistics England and Wales*, Home Office, unless otherwise stated.

• The above information is an extract from a Nacro factsheet. See page 41 for their address details.
© *Nacro, March 2002*

What turns children into criminals?

New research commissioned by the YJB has confirmed the three factors in a child's life most likely to cause him or her to become an offender.

Researchers from Communities that Care analysed a number of different reports and research projects into what caused children to offend and drew conclusions based on all findings. The key risk factors were low achievement in school, family problem behaviour and peer involvement in problem behaviour.

Their report, *The Risk and Protective Factors for Youth Crime – Prevalence, Salience and Reduction*, looked at the influence of family, community, school as well as individual and peer group experience.

Risk factors included poor parental supervision and discipline, family history of criminal activity, living in a disadvantaged neighbourhood, availability of drugs, low achievement in school from primary age and truancy and social alienation.

Low achievement beginning in primary school

The most common risk factors among 11 to 16-year-old offenders were aggressive behaviour (including bullying), low achievement beginning in primary school, family history of problem behaviour, alienation and lack of social commitment, peer attitudes condoning problem behaviour, family conflict, lack of commitment to school (including truancy), friends' involvement in problem behaviour and availability of drugs.

They found the important predictor of being arrested was low achievement at school, with a 90 per cent chance compared to the norm. The second most significant factors were family problem behaviour (62 per cent) and peer involvement in problem behaviour (50 per cent).

Aggressive behaviour and bullying, while one of the most prevalent problems, was reported as the least salient (six per cent).

The report backs the YJB policy of holistic and community intervention as the key to reforming criminals and preventing other children from getting involved in crime.

Benefits of holistic approach

Social bonding, parents, teachers and community leaders who lead by example and hold clearly stated expectations regarding children's behaviour and the promotion within family, school and community of behavioural standards help keep children away from criminal activity. Opportunities for involvement, social and reasoning skills and recognition and due praise are also crucial protective factors.

The report said: 'If it is possible to influence the level of exposure children have to the risk/protective factors through community interventions, we should be able to reduce the prevalence of problem behaviour in those communities . . . the potential benefits of a more holistic, integrated approach that combines "joined-up" planning and working across the fields of health, education and tackling social exclusion cannot be overstated.'

Mark Perfect, chief executive of the YJB, said: 'This valuable report . . . advances the Board's understanding of the nature and scale of the problems associated with youth crime and the evidence in support of various forms of intervention. The report supplies independent advice to inform decisions about where the focus of preventative efforts should be.'

• The above information is an extract from *Youth Justice Board News*, December 2001. See page 41 for their address details.
© *Youth Justice Board*

Young adults

Information from the Howard League for Penal Reform

This information deals with young adults aged between 18 and 21. Offenders aged over 18 are dealt with by the adult courts.

- On 1st September 2000 there were 8,824 young adults in prison.
- 14,264 young men and 879 young women were given a custodial sentence in 1999.
- The number of young adults sent to prison has increased substantially over the last years. 36% more young men, and 144% more young women were sent to prison in 1999 compared to 1994.

What are young adults sent to prison for?

- In 1999, 73% of young adults sentenced to immediate custody had committed non-violent offences (i.e. offences did not involve violence, sex, robbery or drug trafficking).
- The average sentence length in 1999 was 11.4 months for young men and 7.7 months for women.

Young adults on remand

- 16,085 young adults were held on remand during 1999, 14,916 men and 1,169 women.
- Amongst prisoners of all ages, 53% of men and 65% of women remanded in custody in 1999 did not then go on to receive custodial sentences.

Reconviction rates

- Reconviction rates for young adults are very high. 72% of 9,701 males aged 18-20 discharged in 1996 were reconvicted within two years, and 47% of these re-offended so seriously they re-entered prison.

Suicides

- 78% young people aged 18, 19 or 20 killed themselves whilst in prison during the 1990s.

The Howard League believes:

- Prisons are overused. Most young adults in prison have committed non-violent offences and could be more constructively dealt with in the community.
- High reconviction rates indicate that prison does not prevent offending.
- Resources should be diverted into crime prevention and community penalties targeted on the individual needs of each young adult.
- Imprisonment should only be used as a last resort for violent offenders who pose a threat to society.

• The above information is from a factsheet produced by the Howard League for Penal Reform. See their web site at www.howardleague.org Alternatively see page 41 for their address details.

© Howard League for Penal Reform

Statistics on young adults

Number of young adults received into prison custody under sentence

	1994	1995	1996	1997	1998	1999
Men	10476	11175	11810	12525	13245	14264
Women	360	398	498	601	769	879

Young adults sentenced to immediate custody during 1999, England and Wales

Offence	Men	Percentage	Women	Percentage
Violence against the person	2,042	(14%)	139	(16%)
Sexual offences	132	(1%)	2	(0.22%)
Burglary	2,524	(18%)	68	(8%)
Robbery	973	(7%)	39	(4%)
Theft and handling	3,508	(25%)	340	(39%)
Fraud and forgery	170	(1%)	30	(3%)
Drugs offences	697	(5%)	95	(11%)
Other offences	4,403	(28%)	138	(16%)
Offences not recorded	175	(1%)	28	(3%)
Total	**14,264**		**879**	

Source: Prison statistics, England and Wales, 1999. Table 3.11

Young people's attitudes to crime

A MORI survey

To complement the Youth Justice Board's annual quantitative survey of more than 5,000 young people, MORI has conducted a qualitative, in-depth survey of attitudes towards offending of children growing up in England and Wales today.

The study was carried out among young offenders, persistent young offenders and non-offenders from ten to 17, using a mixture of mini-focus groups, one-to-one in-depth interviews and paired interviews. There was a representative spread by age, sex and level of offending. Interviews were carried out in Bradford, Northumberland, Cardiff, Weston-super-Mare, West Sussex, West Suffolk, Stockport, Staffordshire and the London boroughs of Southwark and Lewisham.

The survey found that once a child has committed his or her first offence the barrier against crime was breached, the behaviour became more acceptable to the children and they were likely to slip into a pattern of offending.

'You think you are good smoking and that, when you are about eight or nine. Then you get further up. It goes on to something daft like shop-lifting or something and that is it.'
(15- to 16-year-old male persistent offenders' group, North)

Some boys said they had started to commit 'minor' offences from the age of eight, while for girls the first criminal experience was at 12 years old.

'First thing I ever got done for was burglary. I were about nine or ten.'
(15- to 16-year-old male persistent offenders' group, North)

There were three main factors which influenced children's likelihood to offend: motivators, environmental factors and values.

Motivators (benefits offenders can see for committing crimes, e.g. relieving boredom or frustration, financial gain – for designer items and status as well as for drink or drugs).

'You do it for a laugh.'
(15- to 16-year-old male persistent offenders' group, North)

'That copper up behind you. You get that blood pumping. You know you are going to get chased. That is a rush.'
(15- to 16-year-old male persistent offenders' group, North)

'When I was about nine, I was just f***ing mad and I used to do anything for money.'
(15- to 16-year-old male persistent offenders' group, West)

Environmental factors (beyond young person's control, e.g. living in deprived area or crime hotspot, being with relatives or friends who are offenders). Sometimes offending behaviour is a consequence of family abuse, estrangement or bereavement; sometimes young people attribute offending to lack of parental discipline and even offended with the parent to cement their relationship.

'It is because of the estate we were on. It's a pigsty now. Everywhere you go you can see people out of their face on heroin.'
(13- to 15-year-old male persistent offenders' group, South)

'You just look up to some people and perhaps you should look up to others.'
(17-year-old male persistent offender, depth, North)

'My dad died and then I started going a bit weird in the head. And I started running away. I started robbing.'
(15-year-old female offender, paired depth, South)

'I have been burgling twice when I was with my dad. He smokes [cannabis] as well.'
(16-year-old male persistent offender, depth, North)

Values (not all young people who want money or who are bored commit crimes. Offending appeared to be linked to perceptions of right and wrong and emotional maturity, e.g. if they do not think they are harming anyone they are less likely to see the crime as wrong. Sometimes they will act on impulse if they see an 'opportunity' to offend.)

'I went into the house because it was empty. It was being renovated. I thought there was no one lived in there and I walked in with my friend and I looked in there and there was loads of stuff like widescreen TV, Sky Digital and everything and we thought, "We'll have that, we can sell that".'
(13- to 15-year-old male persistent offenders' group, South)

Substance abuse can affect the young person's decisions, i.e. making them more desperate for money or less considerate of others. In addition, the three factors listed above can affect substance abuse, e.g. where drugs are a factor in a young person's family or environment.

'I probably wouldn't have done half of them things if I weren't pissed.

When I was on Valium I thieved so much alcohol from the shops. You just don't give two shits. And if boys pull up next to you that are stoned in the car, if you're sober you're like, "No, because then I'll get nicked". But if you're pissed you'd be like, "Oh, yes, man, let's go".'

(15-year-old female offender, paired depth, South)

Young offenders tend to view things to be wrong when they can identify a victim. However, they cannot always identify an individual victim even when there is one. (Other young people consider crimes where there is a clear victim, especially if they are physically or emotionally harmed, as 'very bad', whereas drug taking is 'not too bad'.)

'A car is different to a house. Once somebody has been in a house, people think they are going to do it again and they get scared. Whereas with a car nobody is bothered, are they?'

(15- to 16-year-old male persistent offenders' group, North)

The barriers to offending are seen by offenders as being caught and punished, upsetting their families

or the dangers attached to various crimes – with those impacting on themselves or those close to them taken most seriously.

• For the purposes of the survey, 'offenders' are those in contact with Youth Offending Teams (Yots) because they have been caught offending. 'Persistent young offenders' will have committed a number of offences and be well-known to the Yot. 'North' refers to respondents from Northumberland and Bradford, 'West' to Cardiff and Weston-super-Mare, and 'South' to West Sussex, West Suffolk and London.

• The above information is an extract from *Youth Justice Board News*. See page 41 for their address details.

© *Youth Justice Board*

More girls than boys go shoplifting

Girls have overtaken boys in Government shoplifting figures for the first time with the most pronounced difference in the 13 to 15 age group.

Peer pressure, bullying and the need to buy drink and drugs, traditionally seen as influences on young men, are thought to be behind the thefts by schoolgirls, many of whom come from affluent homes.

A charity which works with thousands of people accused of shoplifting – Crisis Counselling for Alleged Shoplifters – has obtained a breakdown of Home Office figures. They show that in 1999, 24,878 men were dealt with by police cautions for shoplifting, compared to 22,956 women. In 2000, the comparable figures were 21,172 and 24,462.

Men outnumber women by about 2-1 in magistrates' and Crown courts where offences by adults can be dealt with by penalties ranging from fines to jail. More than 58,000 shoplifting cases went through the courts in England and Wales last year.

By John Steele, Crime Correspondent

Harry Kauffer, the chairman of CCAS, whose charity deals with up to 3,000 people accused of shop theft each year, said the growing predominance of schoolgirls in the statistics was most worrying. Last year, 2,248 13-year-old girls were cautioned for shoplifting, compared to 1,951 boys. For 14-year-olds, the figures were 2,811 girls and 2,295 boys. There were 2,469 15-year-old girls, against 2,124 boys. Around 1,600 16-year-olds of each sex were cautioned.

Mr Kauffer said that many

Last year, 2,248 13-year-old girls were cautioned for shoplifting, compared to 1,951 boys

youngsters were being sucked into shoplifting without realising that a caution might blight their job prospects. 'It's a concern that young girls have overtaken boys. We never condone premeditated shoplifting but, from those we counsel, there appears to be a number of factors.

'There are those who have a penchant to steal and who do it for a buzz. There are recidivist offenders. But it is mainly about bullying and wanting to be seen to belong to a youth culture in which shoplifting takes place.'

He said some offenders came from troubled backgrounds but about 50 per cent of the shoplifters his charity saw were from affluent families. 'Girls often start with cosmetics but they graduate to trainers, CDs and radios.'

Some parents failed to give teenagers sensible spending money and then turned a blind eye when they arrived home with items which they could not afford.

© *Telegraph Group Limited, London 2002*

Bad girls or bad laws?

YWCA campaigns to end inequality and social injustice experienced by young women offenders. By Clare Dodwell and Lucy Russell

The YWCA believes that young women offenders and those at risk of offending are one of the most vulnerable and socially excluded groups in the country. We are particularly alarmed at the huge increase in the number of young women offenders being sent to prison: an increase of 382% since 1992, despite a decrease in their rates of offending.

Many young women in prison have severe social, emotional, and health problems, often resulting from childhood traumas and instability. For example, almost half of women in prison aged 21 and under have been sexually abused in childhood. 65% of young women aged 15-17 had experienced family breakdown, 57% had been excluded from school or had a history of persistent truancy. 30% of young women aged 16-19 had received previous psychiatric input and 10% had been in psychiatric hospital.

Many young women in prison have children: Home Office research in 1997 revealed that 39% of young women prisoners were mothers. As women are usually the primary carers in the family, if they are imprisoned, the impact on the children is huge. Many are taken into care or have to move to a new area to live with a grandparent or other relative. Their schooling and friendships are often disrupted. Visiting their mother is difficult. She is unlikely to be imprisoned nearby as there are currently only seventeen prisons in the country that take women and only ten that take young offenders.

If a woman is pregnant, there is the possibility of a place in a mother-and-baby unit but as there are only four of these in the whole country places are scarce. Children have to leave when they are 18 months old causing great trauma to the mother.

The experience of being separated from their homes and families has a devastating effect on

women prisoners' mental health. The grief resulting from the loss of contact with children and support networks can be overwhelming. Self-harm as a way of coping with this grief is commonplace. Over 40% of women in prison either self-harm or attempt suicide.

The YWCA is committed to improving the situation for young

We believe that the way to reduce crime and offending by young women is to help them address the underlying causes of their behaviour

---

women offenders and their families. We advocate the use of community sentences for all young women who offend unless they are a genuine risk to the public. A number of our projects work closely with local probation services and provide confidential placements for young women on community service orders. For example, Doncaster YWCA offers one-to-one support from key workers, an on-site crèche and opportunities to access IT training, careers advice, specialist counselling, and a drop-in facility.

We believe that the way to reduce crime and offending by young women is to help them address the underlying causes of their behaviour. These are often linked to painful experiences in childhood and adolescence that have resulted in low self-esteem, poor school achievement, mental and emotional health problems, drug and alcohol problems, drug and alcohol dependence etc. These multiple factors need to be addressed in a supportive and therapeutic setting, using a holistic and needs-led approach. For example, Tonbridge YWCA has recently run a support group for women on probation with crèche provision on site for those with children. The

group followed a structured programme which covered topics such
as drugs and alcohol dependency,
budgeting, healthy lifestyles,
assertiveness and managing conflict.
The women were encouraged to
examine the causes of their offending,
the effect on themselves and others
and looked at ways of avoiding the
triggers for negative behaviour.
Feedback from attendees has been
very positive:

- *'it was a very low time both
  emotionally and physically for me
  and this group helped me turn my
  life around'*
- *'the groups helps to look at yourself
  rather than the crime therefore if
  you feel a better person the chances
  of re-offending are low . . . The
  group has helped me find myself
  again. I do not want to lose that.'*

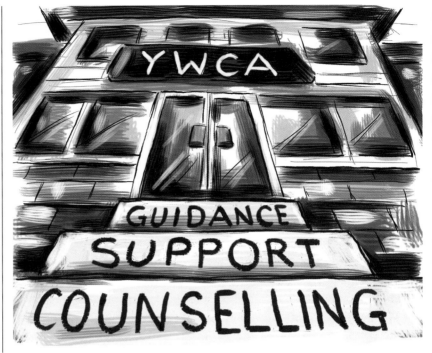

Case study

S was convicted, with a female associate, for mugging an elderly lady. The
courts dealt quite harshly with the pair and although she had a small son,
S served about a year in prison. Her son was taken into foster care and
visited his mother infrequently. When S was released on a tag she was
about as nervous as any young woman I have come across. She could hardly
lift her head. Due to the tag she was on a curfew which lasted from 7am to
7pm. This did not add to her feeling of well-being.

Gradually she began to get her life back together. She began to talk
about her experiences in prison, what it was like and how she had felt. I
gained the impression that she had felt a kind of security in there and a
sense of comradeship that she had not previously experienced as her home
life and childhood had been fairly chaotic.

Her son was returned to her and during the summer she came with us on
trips to local parks and on one occasion to a craft centre that had a
children's play area with a ball pool. S took her son into the pool but had
no idea how to play with him. One of the staff went in too and set the
example, to which S responded. It was such a poignant moment.

At the end of the summer S obtained her own council house. We helped
her to get established, supported her in dealings with the council, utility
suppliers etc. and she seemed to be settling in well. We continued to
support her on a floating basis visiting her regularly and encouraging her
to visit the YWCA. However, at around this time, S had met and become
very attached to another young woman. Together they went on drinking
sessions and began to get in trouble with the police. The final straw came
when they fell through a shop window and stole what they could pick up.
S took the blame and was sent back to prison as she was still on licence. We
visited her and once again supported her on her release. She managed to
hold onto her tenancy as her sentence had been short and soon regained
custody of her son, but once again she faced a long struggle to get her life
back together.

*Stories such as these are common among the young women offenders we work
with. At a national level, in our policy and campaigns work, we are committed
to changing things for the better for these young women and their children. We
are currently playing an active part in the newly formed Gender and Justice
Policy Network, co-ordinated by the Fawcett Society, challenging and influencing
government policy and strategy on women offenders.*

Other YWCA projects offer
support to young women in prison
and on their release. For example,
Crewe YWCA provides guidance
and support to women leaving prison
on matters such as finding
accommodation, claiming benefits,
and accessing training and
employment and parenting support.
The case study on this page written
by the project worker tells the story
of one young woman they have
worked with.

• The YWCA is a leading women's
organisation and one of the oldest in
the UK. Through our network of
Youth and Community projects in
England and Wales we provide
services to women who are
experiencing disadvantage to help
them identify and realise their full
potential. Through our Policy and
Campaigns work, we are committed
to raising the social and political
profile of young women's issues and
experiences and bring about changes
in social policy that will a have a
positive impact on the lives of girls
and young women.

• The above information appeared
in the October 2001 edition of
Action for Prisoners' Families, the
newsletter of the Federation of
Prisoners' Families Support
Groups.

See page 41 for YWCA of Great
Britain's address and contact details.
© YWCA of Great Britain

Violent crime by the young

Gang members by the age of eight, 'hard core' criminals by 14

The only solution to violent crime by the young is to introduce special tribunals to get them off the streets fast, Sir John Stevens, the Met's Commissioner, tells Alasdair Palmer and David Bamber.

Two weeks ago, at 10 o'clock in the evening, Tim Robinson was parking his car just outside his home in Battersea, south London. His girlfriend Jemma Joyce was on the pavement, guiding him into a small parking space.

Mr Robinson, a 27-year-old estate agent, then saw two youths go up to his girlfriend and start remonstrating with her. He got out to find out what they wanted.

As he walked up to them, the youths leapt towards him and stabbed him six times in his face and body. Mr Robinson died of his wounds three days later.

His murderers were both in their teens. Their crime was shocking – horrible in its casual brutality and completely futile violence.

The youth and cruelty of Mr Robinson's killers is evidence of a horrifying trend in Britain's cities: an increasing number of violent crimes are being committed by children.

They are not old enough to vote, to drink or to drive legally: indeed, they are scarcely old enough to take full responsibility for anything they do.

The courts regard them as 'minors'. They should be in school getting a basic education. Instead, they are out robbing, and sometimes killing, on the streets.

There have been a series of murders by teenagers in the past few years: Stephen Lawrence, Damilola Taylor, Ricky Everitt, Jamie Robe and Philip Lawrence are just some of those who were killed by individuals who were still legally children when they committed murder.

While murders by teenagers are still mercifully rare, violent street crimes – attacks, robberies, stabbings – are most certainly not.

Mr Robinson's murderers ran off towards Doddington, a sprawling council estate known to the local police as a haven for thugs and yobs who rob and attack people on nearby streets.

One 45-year-old mother was recently robbed at knife-point in the area. Her assailants cut her hand as she handed over her purse, clearly, she says, 'just for the hell of it' – the stabbing had no purpose.

While murders by teenagers are still mercifully rare, violent street crimes – attacks, robberies, stabbings – are most certainly not

---

The victim recognised one of her attackers. 'He used to play with my son,' she said. 'He was so friendly when he was little. He's now 14 and he was so brutal, and so nasty . . . he was just out of control.'

What turned the 'so friendly' child into the 'so brutal, so nasty' teenager? Academics cite the overwhelming statistical association between violent, abusive teenagers and children who have been abandoned, abused and attacked themselves.

But to the police, the most pressing difficulty is finding some way to deal with the havoc that violent children are causing. 'The problem is extremely serious,' says Sir John Stevens, Commissioner of the Metropolitan Police.

'Our investigations suggest that there are between 20 and 30 almost wild children in each inner London borough. They do not respect, or even seem to understand, the most basic standards.'

There was a case recently, for instance, in which a group of teenage thugs laughed as they robbed and mugged a young child with cerebral palsy. His desperate and pathetic cries had no effect whatever on them: they just found tormenting him funny.

'These young criminals have no fear at all,' continues Sir John. 'No fear of the law, no fear of the police and no fear at the prospect of prison.'

Commander Andre Baker, of the Met's Serious Crime Group, echoes Sir John: 'We are developing a gang culture among young kids in Britain.

'It isn't as bad as what happens in America, at least not yet. But children as young as eight are getting involved in gangs and introduced to crime.

'They are being bullied by older children, and quickly coming to realise that the way to protect yourself from older thugs is to imitate them. They join gangs, they encourage each other to act tough, and they start thieving.

'That's how the escalation starts. It can end with violence on the streets, even with murder.'

By the age of 13, the hard core have started to graduate to violent street robbery.

Ebeneezer Gorazeb, 33, the treasurer of the Doddington Estate Resource Centre, knows from experience that if you are going to reform child criminals, you have to catch them between about eight and ten because, he says, 'by the age of 14 or 15, it is already too late'.

They are already fixed on fast money and the spurious glamour of violent crime and can't be persuaded out of it.

Indeed, last week the Office for Standards in Education reported that as many as 10,000 children, mostly aged 14 or 15, were missing from the state school system altogether. Some may be working but others, Ofsted admitted, were probably out committing crime.

Most car-jacking is done by youngsters between the ages of 13 and 18. 'They don't know what civilised standards are,' says Commander Baker.

'They don't really have any family attachments. Many of them show more affection for their gang than for their own families – which may not be entirely surprising, considering how their families may have treated them.

'They don't have any respect for authority. I'm not sure they even know what it is. They've been excluded from school and through the criminal justice system numerous times already. But nothing has had any effect. To them, it's all just a huge joke.

'They know exactly how to play the system when we arrest them,' Commander Baker continues.

'You may only be dealing with a 14-year-old, but he can be an expert at intimidating witnesses, delaying identity parades, finding ways to postpone court hearings – from asking for medical reports on his own fitness to plead, to simply failing to turn up.'

He cites the case of Tao Jones, a gang member sentenced for murder last month, to illustrate the widespread contempt felt by youngsters for the criminal justice system which is supposed to be reforming, or at least intimidating, them.

'When he was arrested,' Commander Baker remembers, 'Jones just smiled and said, "You'll never get the evidence". He clearly wasn't in the least bothered, even though he knew that his victim's girlfriend had seen the murder.'

Jones was certain he could terrify her into silence. To her great credit, the witness was not intimidated: she came forward, and her evidence convicted him. She is now in a witness protection scheme which has involved a change of identity.

The courts do not seem to recognise how dedicated to criminality some of the youngsters are. 'Time after time,' says Sir John wearily, 'the courts grant bail to these young thugs. And the moment they are out, they offend again.'

In one case in Basingstoke, Hants, a group of 14-year-olds besieged a couple in their own home. They kicked the door and hurled stones.

When the home-owner confronted his tormentors, they punched and kicked him to the ground. They did the same to his wife when she tried to come to his aid. The children were arrested and interviewed by the police, who were then forced to release them on bail.

No one has any doubt that all of those children went straight back to committing violent crimes on the street.

Sir John is emphatic that a radical solution is needed if the problem of rising violence by children is to be tackled.

'The present system is failing everybody,' he says. 'It doesn't allow us to protect the public from these criminals, and it doesn't allow anyone to help the young criminals reform in any way.

'What we need is a completely new, specially-designed, fast-track system to deal with these kids because the normal court procedures have proved themselves quite inappropriate.

'They are just too slow, and too cumbersome to deal with the problem we face.

'We need a special judicial system, with special tribunals, set up specifically to deal with these violent criminals so that we can get them off the streets and start trying to do something with them which will stop them offending.'

There would be a great deal of opposition to such a plan from those who have a vested interest in continuing the present system: the probation service and lawyers.

At present, however, there is a more fundamental problem that the courts frequently order the release of child offenders because there is nowhere to put them.

Sir John's solution is straightforward: 'We need hundreds of new secure places in young offender institutions to keep these thugs off the streets,' he insists.

'I have made it clear to the Home Office that we need the new places if we are to keep violent children off the streets. Of course it will not be cheap.

'But if you factor in the huge financial costs – never mind the human costs – of letting these kids out on the streets as we do at the moment, it is quite obvious that finding an appropriate way to keep them off the streets is going to save everyone money.'

Sir John and his supporters in the police have yet to succeed in persuading the Government to take the radical action needed to deal with dangerously violent teenagers.

He is, however, certain of one point: if nothing is done, the problem is going to get much, much worse.

Huge rise in mobile phone thefts from children

Home Office study urges manufacturers to help curb a crime trend that leaves teenagers at particular risk

By Alan Travis, Home Affairs Editor

Up to half a million young people aged between 11 and 15 fell victim to a mobile phone theft last year, according to an official Home Office research report to be published today. The study also estimates that the overall number of stolen mobiles is more than double the 330,000 officially recorded by the police.

While about 1% of all adults had a mobile stolen last year, the chance of becoming a victim rises more than fivefold for those aged 11-16, with 5% of Britain's younger teenagers reporting that they had their phone stolen at least once. For those aged under 16 and living in deprived areas in big cities, the figure rises to 12%.

The report is also sceptical about possible methods of curbing the problem, to be canvassed today by Home Office ministers. And it found that the mobile phone manufacturers have so far failed to come up with a way of disabling a stolen handset at a cost which they are prepared to pay.

The researchers also cast doubt on the value of a technique known as 'bombing', whereby the police bombard stolen mobiles with a continuous flow of text messages. Members of a group of young offenders were said by researchers to be 'bemused' by this proposal: 'In their view, avoiding it would simply be a matter of stealing another phone on the expectation that its loss would not be reported, or that the police would not be able to keep up.'

Crime trends

The Home Office study by Victoria Harrington and Pat Mayhew confirms it is the sharp rise in mobile phone thefts in the past two years that is mainly fuelling an alarming rise in street robbery, at a time when other types of crime – including violent crime – are going down. The researchers suggest that street robberies would have 'levelled off' were it not for the explosion in mobile thefts.

> **While about 1% of all adults had a mobile stolen last year, the chance of becoming a victim rises more than fivefold for those aged 11-16**

The researchers qualify this by saying that the high number of mobile phone thefts may simply reflect the fact that mobiles are now prominent among the smaller, higher value 'stealable' items that people carry. When incidents in which only a mobile phone was taken are excluded from robbery trend figures, the robbery rate over the past two years has risen by 8%, compared with the 13% increase recorded by the police. In addition, the proportion of robberies involving mobiles has soared from 8% three years ago to 28% last year. Such robberies now make up 36% of all robberies in London and 41% of those in Birmingham.

Robber profiles

The official study says that the most likely phone robber is male, younger than most other kinds of robbers, with most aged only 14 to 17, and – in five out of the seven police areas studied – most probably black, and operating in a gang. Fewer than 10% of mobile phone thefts are carried out by teenage girls.

While the majority of those accused of being phone robbers are black (rising to 71% in London) there is some variation around the country. In Birmingham 34% of suspects were Asian and 54% black, and in Stockport 76% of suspects were white.

The research also shows mobile phone robbery is predominantly a male-on-male and black-on-white teenage crime in the four city centres studied. 'Young male phone users have cause to be the most wary. Probably, though, women and girls are more vulnerable to theft from the person, which often involves thefts from bags. Risks of unattended phones are likely to be fairly equal.

'A third of incidents against women involved female offenders or mixed groups although this was rare when men were targeted. Women, then, have cause to be more wary than men about the groups in which girls or women act suspiciously. They still, though, should be more wary about men.'

For adults the street robbery risk is lower, and they are as likely to lose a mobile when it is left in the car, when their home is broken into or when they leave the phone elsewhere. The researchers speculate that the street robbery risk facing teenagers is much higher because they are more likely to be out and about, and are less careful with their phones.

The researchers point out that this explosion in mobile thefts is mainly down to the fact that they are 'small, fairly valuable items for which ready resale markets exist among those without a phone, or with an old model. One market will be dubious outlets at which phones can be reprogrammed and possibly sent abroad to countries with growing demand.'

It is easy for potential thieves to spot someone with a phone in the street, with a quarter of all phone robberies involving somebody using their mobile or having it on display.

For the group of convicted thieves in Feltham young offenders' institution, mobile phones were viewed as an indispensable and a technologically fascinating crutch. They claimed the loss of a mobile was one of the worst elements of imprisonment. The Feltham offenders also testified that the value of the handset was more important than the free phone calls, and said the phones could be sold for between £10 and £60, depending on the model. 'The fact that new Sim cards can be got easily and cheaply was also important for those wanting to keep or pass on a "flashy" phone.'

But some police officers believed that the phones are stolen less for their value than as a system by which gangs of teenage boys establish territorial rights and 'show who's who' by penalising other street users, especially other teenagers, by 'taxing' them through phone thefts.

Finally the authors ask whether the tide has already turned in mobile phone thefts, due to the greater care being taken by phone owners, and because mobiles are so commonplace that they are now less of a 'must have' item. But they conclude that any new generation of phones could well generate a crime harvest such as the one that occurred each time a new car stereo model came onto the market.

They suggest the main moral to date is that the phone manufacturers should have thought more in advance about the crime potential. 'Hindsight then tells us that better security needs to be a key issue for the next generation of phones.'

Young offenders 'denied fresh air'

By Alan Travis, Home Affairs Editor

Some inmates in youth jails hardly ever get out into the sunlight and fresh air and are living in conditions which fall short of international standards, according to research by the Howard League for Penal Reform.

The claim that some youths only got to breathe fresh air when they were moved between units was made in the first two of a series of research studies into conditions inside young offenders' institutions.

The inquiries at Lancaster Farms, near Lancaster, and Castington, Northumberland, claimed that boys suffered widespread bullying, lack of specialist help, and were given little preparation for their release.

The Howard League said that 55% of inmates at Castington said they had been involved in a bullying incident in the previous week. Some officers were dismissive to children who harmed themselves with one officer referring to a boy who persistently cut himself as 'Slasher'.

At Lancaster Farms the penal reformers were alarmed to find how little access there was to daylight and the open air: 'Boys only have access to fresh air when they are moving between units. The lack of access to natural air and sunlight is likely to impact on the boys' mental and physical well-being,' said their report.

'This lack of access is very worrying. Adolescents have a lot of energy that needs to be burned up or it may manifest itself in frustration and aggression.'

Charlotte Day of the Howard League said the reports showed that since the youth justice board had taken over the running of institutions for under-18s last year there had been improvements but standards still fell short of those laid down in the United Nations convention on the rights of the child.

'Children in prison may have committed crimes but they are still children. They should be entitled to the same level of care provided for children in every other setting.'

Martin Narey, the director general of the prison service, said that he did not believe there was a prison service anywhere in the world which could better British standards of care for 'this frequently volatile and unpredictable age group'.

He said that Sir David Ramsbotham, the chief inspector of prisons, had said that Lancaster Farms was a 'centre of excellence' and had also praised Castington.

Conditions for child prisoners breach international standards

Information from the Howard League for Penal Reform

New research released today by the Howard League reveals that conditions for children in prison fail to meet international standards.

The research examined conditions for young people aged 15 to 17 at Lancaster Farms and Castington young offender institutions. It reveals that whilst there have been improvements in the range of activities available to young prisoners, the quality of care provided for them still fails to meet standards laid out in the United Nations Convention on the Rights of the Child and other international standards.

Amongst the issues of concern highlighted in the reports are:

Lack of specialist training for staff
Prison officers have almost no specialist training to deal with young people, let alone children in prison many of whom are damaged or disturbed.

Prison units too large to provide individual care
Boys are held in units of 60. Staff at all levels felt that this was too many and were frustrated that they were unable to give children the level of support they could see was needed.

Limited access to daylight and open air
Boys only have access to fresh air when they are moving between units. The lack of access to natural air and sunlight is likely to impact on the boys' mental and physical well-being.

Difficulties controlling bullying
Bullying, particularly at Castington, was widespread. The prevalence of bullying is influenced by situational factors – in particular boredom, lack of supervision, and restricted access to goods – and the existence of a culture amongst the boys which supports it.

Lack of preparation for release
Very little work was done with boys in order to prepare them for release, and the education and training boys do in prison is not linked into resources in the community. Everything done in prison should be seen as preparation for the future rather than just a means of passing time.

Speaking today, Charlotte Day, author of the reports, said: 'Children in prison may have committed crimes but they are still children. They should be entitled to the same level of care and protection provided for children in every other setting. The UK ratified the United Nations Convention on the Rights of the Child in 1991 and, as a signatory, is committed to meeting the minimum standards outlined in the treaty.'

'Recent changes to the youth justice system, including the introduction of the Youth Justice Board and the imposition of standards, have improved access to activities for children – but the fundamental character of prison is unchanged. Prisons are institutions designed for security rather than care and the Howard League is concerned that they still fail to meet the needs of children.'

- The reports *Children in Prison: provision and practice at Lancaster Farms* and *Children in Prison: provision and practice at Castington* are available from the Howard League priced £5 each.

> **'Prisons are institutions designed for security rather than care and the Howard League is concerned that they still fail to meet the needs of children'**

Notes

1. Lancaster Farms is situated just outside Lancaster. It holds up to 130 juveniles (aged 15-17) and up to 366 young adults (aged 18-20). Castington is in Northumberland. It holds up to 280 juveniles and up to 120 young adults. Both prisons hold young people under sentence and on remand.

2. On 30 June 2001 there were 2,478 young people aged 15 to 17 in prison in England and Wales.

3. During 1999, 68% of children sentenced to immediate custody had committed non-violent offences (i.e. offences did not involve violence, sex, robbery or drug trafficking).

4. Thirteen prisons are designated to hold juveniles. Ten of these also hold young adults but in separate units to prevent mixing between the two groups. Conditions for juveniles are significantly better than for young adults.

5. On 1 April 2000, the youth justice board assumed responsibility for purchasing and commissioning places in prison. On this date new standards for the care of juveniles in prison were also implemented (prison service order 4950), and a new custodial sentence (the detention and training order) was introduced.

6. These are the first two in a series of reports the Howard League will be producing on conditions for children in prison.

- The above information is from the Howard League for Penal Reform's web site: www.howardleague.org Alternatively, see page 41 for their address details.

© The Howard League for Penal Reform

Time to educate the criminals?

By Kirstine Hansen

Facts about current levels of crime

Before coming to power in 1997, Prime Minister Tony Blair promised to be tough on crime and touch on the cause of crime. But as politicians gear up for the next general election, widely expected in 2001, the Blair government finds itself struggling to deal with a crime wave. Figures published in July 2000 show a rise in crime which has sparked new public concern about the measures used to combat criminal activity. Kirstine Hansen reports on new Centre for Economic Performance (CEP) research on the role of education.

In the year to March 2000, 5.3 million offences were recorded by the police in England and Wales. 83% of all crimes involved property: 50% of these were thefts; 20% were thefts of and from vehicles; and a further 8% were burglaries. 13% of all crimes were violent crimes; the remaining 4% included drug offences, public order offences and crimes involving the prevention of the course of justice.

But the crime statistics only tell us what crimes were reported to the police: crucially, they do not tell us who committed the crimes. For that information we must look to the figures relating to those found guilty of or cautioned for indictable offences. (Since not all crimes are solved, these figures only relate to a proportion of all crimes reported.) In 1997, there were 509,000 offenders: the vast majority – 82% – were male and about 25% were under 25. Research shows that involvement in crime tends to rise and peak in the mid to late teens and early twenties. It is the high level of youth crime, taking place at a time when the proportion of young people in the population is declining which has become the focus of much public concern and, in turn, the efforts of policymakers.

Why the young turn to crime

In trying to combat the problem of youth crime, we first need to establish why young people are more likely to commit crimes. Whilst they are young most individuals have no strong sense of self-identity; much of their behaviour is based on trying to achieve short-term desires. Delinquency could simply be a way of getting 'kicks', having a laugh or relieving boredom. Peer pressure may increase delinquency as youngsters are encouraged to prove themselves and show loyalty to their peers. At this stage most youngsters feel little pressure to conform to societal norms which means social controls are unable to deter them from breaking the law. What's more, young people tend to be protected from harsh punishment in the criminal justice system. This combination of factors predicts a higher involvement in crime for young people.

But as young people grow older, they begin to be influenced by a series of factors which discourage them from breaking the law. They start to think of much delinquent behaviour as childish. As they move from dependence to independence, leaving school and the parental home and entering the labour market, getting married and starting families of their own, young people begin to develop ties to society and attachments to social institutions such as the family, the labour market and the community. These factors, coupled with the possibility of more severe legal sanctions, all encourage a lower crime rate, at least in public, as young people move towards adulthood.

Why aren't all young people criminals?

All this explains why on average young people are more attracted to crime than older people. It doesn't explain why two people of the same age don't display the same propensity to become criminals – if they did, then by definition all young people would turn to crime. This has led social scientists to explore what other factors, besides age, are important. One key factor (though not the only one) is of course exposure to the education system – a child's experience of school. New findings suggest this may play an important role in determining the likelihood of a young person's involvement in crime.

A 1998 report by HM Chief Inspectorate of Prisons showed that there were 10,570 young people under the age of 22 in the custody of the prison services in England and Wales in 1997. This represented a

5% increase on the previous year. The report points out 'most of the youngsters had been failed by the education system'. Around two-thirds of these youths had no formal qualifications, many had regularly played truant from school and over 50% had been excluded (or left voluntarily) before the age of 16.

These findings reinforce an important link between education and offending which has been found in many empirical studies. An American study in 1999 found that high-school graduation reduced criminal participation among young males in the US, even after differences in ability were controlled for. It also found that young male high-school graduates were 30% less likely to earn an income from crime than those who did not graduate. Moreover, high-school graduation reduced the probability of being arrested by around 60% and incarceration by between 85-95%.

The links between education and crime

Education can affect the likelihood of offending in a variety of ways. The most cynical explanation is that whilst youngsters are at school, they are being kept off the streets. This separates them from the most delinquent peers (who are likely to be absent from school) and enforces some level of discipline upon them. At the same time they are encouraged by the idea of meritocracy to have aspirations, to create goals which by working hard at school they will be able to achieve. This encourages children to develop a stake in their own future and in society more generally. All these factors would tend to reduce the involvement of young people in crime.

More importantly, though, education encourages children to develop skills and acquire knowledge and training which will affect their future success in life. Their ability to communicate and forge relationships, the choices they make at the end of compulsory education, the jobs they will do and the wages they will receive over their lifetime potentially depend on they skills they acquire whilst still at school. If children want to maximise their future success they will be less likely to offend as youngsters. And if they secure successful jobs with good wages as a result of their educational success they will also be less likely to offend as adults.

New research

Focusing on the importance played by education this current research uses self-reported data collected from young men aged 16-25 in England and Wales to examine the crime-age profiles of two groups: those who leave school at 16 and those who stay on past the compulsory school-leaving age. Findings show that the two groups have significantly different crime-age profiles; but that the gap between the two profiles can be accounted for by differences across the two groups in a number of observable factors related to the labour market, education, family, individual and the area/neighbourhood in which the young men live. Of these, the three most important are whether an individual lives with their parents, family contact with the police and school truancy.

The crime-age profile

If the age at which an individual leaves school has no link with their involvement in criminal activity then we would expect the crime-age profiles of the two groups to be essentially the same. Figure 1 shows clearly that this is not the case. For those who stay on at school, criminal activity is almost non-existent by the age of 25; for those who leave school at 16, there is no real decline in the crime rate from the age of 22 onwards.

Policy implications

These findings have potentially important policy implications: obliging people to stay on at school may affect the crime rate. Unfortunately, the issue isn't quite so clear cut. We need to know why these crime-age profiles are so different before the correct policy response can be determined.

In order to do this, other variables which might influence the crime-age distribution for the two groups are examined to see what impact they have on the crime-age profiles. If any of these variables are able to account for a significant proportion of the difference in the crime-age distributions between the two groups, the two distributions would become more similar. If any or all completely explain the difference in the profiles then the gap will be completely reduced and the two groups will have the same crime-age profiles.

Other factors which affect the crime-age profile

Where people live

Crime and delinquency are unevenly distributed. Evidence from the *British Crime Survey* suggests that over half of all property crime and a third of all victims of property crimes are found in just a fifth of communities in England and Wales. In the 1990s those in the worst crime areas suffered twice as much property crime as anyone else in England and Wales. The police statistics reveal similar trends. Police force areas that include large urban conurbations have the highest rates of recorded crime. In the year to March 2000 Metropolitan forces recorded an annual rise of 7.2% compared to the 0.9% recorded by non-metropolitan forces. The greatest increases were in the West Midlands area, which saw a 16% increase, and London with the Metropolitan and the City of London forces recording an increase of nearly 13%, followed closely by West Midlands with an 11% increase. These forces together with the City of London, Greater Manchester and Merseyside recorded increases totalling 190,000.

Within areas crime rates are highest in inner-city areas, those with a high proportion of social housing and poorly maintained areas. These patterns have been accentuated by recent trends in crime prevention and control which have encouraged individual self-protection, home security devices, neighbourhood watch schemes, insurance and private policing which lead to increased crime in poorer areas, where individuals cannot afford to protect themselves.

Their experience of school

It is not difficult to see that schools influence children's behaviour outside as well as inside the school, particularly in relation to delinquency. Not only is the age an individual leaves school important, their attendance, whether they have been excluded and the qualifications they gain are all differentially associated with offending.

Individual characteristics

Empirical work has shown that a number of individual characteristics are associated with offending. For example, crimes rates are higher for non-whites than for white people. According to the Home Office 18% of the prison population of England and Wales in 1997 were non-white men, even though non-whites accounted for only 6% of the total population of England and Wales. Marriage has also been found to discourage involvement in crime. Young people who have good relationships with their parents are less likely to be involved in criminal activity, while those who have run away from home are more likely to be offenders – as are youths living away from home.

Which family they come from

Delinquents disproportionately come from lower-class and low-income families. Their parents, if in employment, tend to be in low-paid manual jobs. Delinquents are also more likely to have convicted parents or delinquent older siblings.

And the labour market

Several studies have examined the link between the labour market and crime. Although there is as yet no consensus, many found that, at least to some extent, crime is related to unemployment, inequality and low wages.

Which factors matter most?

When all these factors are taken into account, the crime-age profiles are indeed substantially altered. Figure 2 shows that the two profiles now look very similar. They completely come together at ages 16, 24 and 25; with only a slight gap between the two profiles from 17 to 23. All the variables combined account for 90% of the overall gap.

Of course some of these characteristics matter more than others. Table 1 shows that the most important set of variables explaining the gap on average are school variables which account for approximately 46% of the gap overall; family variables which explain 26% of the gap; and individual variables 27%. But we can also see from Table 1 that there are variations across ages. For example, individual variables explain very little of the gap at the younger end of the age profile (4% of the gap at age 16), but much of the gap between the ages of 20 and 22. This is perhaps linked to the movement away from the parental home, towards

Statistics

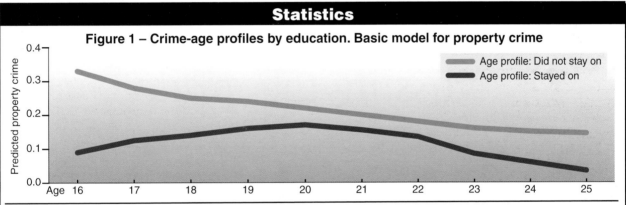

Figure 1 – Crime-age profiles by education. Basic model for property crime

Age profile: Did not stay on
Age profile: Stayed on

Table 1 – Proportion of the gap in the crime-age profiles accounted for by the inclusion of additional variables – Property offences

Age	16	17	18	19	20	21	22	23	24	25	Mean
Gap	.226	.159	.103	.063	.043	.036	.046	.64	.85	.102	**.092**
% explained by area/neighbourhood	10.2	11.9	15.5	17.5	17.1	8.3	0	0	1.2	6.9	**9.0%**
% explained by school vars.	21.7	30.2	44.7	69.8	100.0	105.6	97.8	56.3	44.7	42.2	**45.7%**
% explained by family vars.	25.2	-1.3	-34.0	-68.3	-75.6	-16.7	65.2	100.0	122.4	105.9	**26.1%**
% explained by individual vars.	4.0	6.9	17.5	39.7	70.7	83.3	65.2	45.3	38.8	40.2	**27.2%**
% explained by labour market vars.	11.9	10.1	0	-22.2	-58.5	-69.4	-37.0	-7.8	14.1	23.5	**-1.2%**
% explained by all variables	104.4	96.9	82.5	60.3	39.0	50.0	80.4	95.3	101.2	100.0	**90.2%**

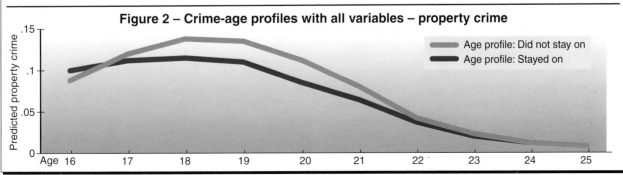

Figure 2 – Crime-age profiles with all variables – property crime

Age profile: Did not stay on
Age profile: Stayed on

setting up new families and having children in the early twenties.

Being more specific

So we know that school variables, family and individual variables account for the largest proportion of the gap between the profiles for those with more education and those with less. But we would also like to know which specific factors within these groups are most important. Findings show that at school, truancy is the most important factor. Those who have played truant are 14 percentage points more likely to commit property crimes. Within the family, it's whether an individual's family has had contact with the police: those with family members who have had contact with the police are 1927 percentage points more likely to commit offences. And of the individual characteristics, what matters most is whether an individual lives with their parents at age 16. Those who do are 8 percentage points less likely to commit crimes.

The implications for policy

There's little doubt that these findings have important implications for long-term efforts to reduce crime committed by young people. One obvious solution might be to encourage more young people to stay on at school which would facilitate a jump across educational profiles. The recent introduction of educational maintenance allowance for children staying on at school may go some of the way to encourage children, particularly those from lower-income families, to stay in education. However, we do not yet know enough to know if this would work, since we do not know whether it is the acquisition of qualifications or merely the act of staying on at school which discourages criminal involvement.

The other route for policy-makers to explore, is to look at policies aimed at the specific factors which close the gap between the two crime-age profiles. This may include policies to reduce truancy such as the publication of truancy league tables or improving facilities for less academic children in order to maintain their interest in education. Policy initiatives aimed at reducing child poverty, such as Sure Start, are also likely to help, by focusing on improving conditions for the poorest children in areas such as health, learning and family and community bonds. These measures are likely to encourage and motivate children better for education, but also reduce the financial burden placed on families where children remain in education past the age of 16.

Neither approach offers a quick fix to the problem of youth crime. But through a combination of policies aimed at improving conditions in a number of areas it is likely that youth crime can be reduced over time.

• Kirstine Hansen is in the Department of Sociology at the London School of Economics. A more detailed account of her research in this area (Kirstine Hansen: Education and the crime-age profile) is forthcoming in the *British Journal of Criminology*.

© *Kirstine Hansen*

Missing the grade

Information from the Howard League for Penal Reform

There is a long tradition of prison as a place where people can be offered new chances in education and training to help them avoid further offending when released. Nowhere is this more important than for those so young that they are in prison when they should be in school.

Many children in prison have poor educational backgrounds – they have often missed school because of exclusion or truancy; they are more likely to have low basic skills or special educational needs. Our research has confirmed this basic picture but we also found that nearly a third of the boys to whom we talked were sufficiently able to take GCSE or GNVQ exams.

For those with poor educational backgrounds, prison can at least offer an opportunity to reconnect with education and to tackle some of their basic educational problems. Under the Detention and Training Order a new emphasis has been placed on education and the Prison Service has issued guidance which states that prisons should: 'deliver an education programme which identifies the needs of individuals and comprises nationally accredited courses which help prevent further offending by preparing each individual for a return to education and/or training or employment on release'.

Our evidence, from interviews with over 80 boys in prison, is that many – and not only the most able – would welcome this.

But our research also shows that the current system for the education of school-aged boys in prison does not match up to these aspirations.

It falters at the point at which boys enter prison. Too little information comes through to prisons about the educational needs of boys. The assessment tests used by the Prison Service are geared to adults, not those of school age.

There is then little scope for meeting the individual needs of boys while they are in prison. A system of performance targets focuses attention on a narrow range of accredited courses – these do not meet the needs of the less able, who require different specialist help; they undermine the more able, who see their opportunities to take GCSE exams frustrated by undemanding teaching.

The curriculum on offer is often narrow. Equipment and facilities are lacking – access to computers is restricted because of security, while opportunities for vocational training often remain available only to older prisoners.

The return to education in the community is not always smooth. Education staff do not always take part in planning for release; opportunities for temporary release to provide transition are not available; careers advice is patchy. Most worrying – though outside the formal scope of our research – was the suggestion that many people find it difficult to find a place in education when released.

Educational contracts, which are largely with further education colleges, create a number of problems:

They require standard, and large, classes, making individual learning difficult.

Teaching staff are largely FE trained; they do not have the training or experience needed to teach younger pupils with special needs, nor are they provided with professional development to help them do so.

Throughout our research we were impressed by the commitment of staff in the prison education system to make it work. We saw many isolated examples of innovative practice – we give details of these in the main body of the report. But our overall conclusion is that the system itself is in need of reform.

Key recommendations

A prison sentence for children of statutory school age is disruptive to their education and has long-term effects on their attainment and future employment. Sending children of school age to prison is detrimental to their education.

Children of statutory school age in prison should have the same entitlement to education as young people in the community. Legislation such as the Education Act 1993, the Education Act 1996, the Code of Practice for students with special educational needs and the Children Act 1989 should apply to children in prison.

Children with special educational needs in prison should have the same access to teaching support and specialised resources as children in the community. They should be entitled to additional funding from the LEA to meet their special educational needs.

Teaching staff working with school-aged children in juvenile prisons should be DfEE qualified and have experience of teaching school-age children.

LEAs should retain responsibility for children when they are sent to prison. They should ensure that prisons receive accurate and detailed information on a child's previous education. They should ensure that all children of school age released from prison have the opportunity of a full-time educational placement at an educational facility that meets their needs.

Education must be seen as more than the time spent in classrooms in prison. It must be about re-engaging the young person in mainstream education and training. Education for children in prison must be seen as part of a broader system which includes the educational opportunities available after release and which is focused on the needs and interests of the individual boy.

The contractual arrangements for providing education for children in prison need to be reviewed. Arrangements for education, PE and vocational training need to be brought into line and linked to the provision available for children outside the prison system.

• The above information is the executive summary of *Missing the Grade – Education for Children in Prison* by the Howard League for Penal Reform, 55pp, £10.00, ISBN 090368357-1. For details of ordering the report, please contact the Howard League for Penal Reform at the address shown on page 41.

© *Howard League for Penal Reform*

Colin's story

Colin is 15 and had been attending secondary school before being sentenced to prison for 3 years. He had been studying for his GCSEs in English, maths, science and geography and a GNVQ in IT. Colin had completed nearly a year of coursework for these subjects. He enjoyed school and spoke positively about his teachers.

Colin was sent to a prison in the south of England, 80 miles from his home town. He was keen to be able to continue with his examination work whilst in prison and wanted someone from the YOT or the prison to contact his school to ask the teachers to send work in. This had not happened.

The breakdown in communication between the school, the YOT and the prison meant Colin missed the registration date for the GCSE exams. The head of education at the prison, realising that Colin was an able student capable of achieving Grades A-C in his GCSEs, enrolled him for the next GCSE sitting.

Colin was moved to another juvenile prison 3 weeks before he was due to sit the exams. The head of education was given no warning about Colin's move. He had not been consulted and it appeared other prison staff were not aware that Colin was due to sit his GCSEs. Colin told us: 'I was moved because it would be nearer to my house but this stopped me sitting my GCSEs. I wasn't warned about the move.'

It was not possible to re-register Colin at the new prison as the examination board required advance notification. Colin told us the education department at his new juvenile prison was trying to enrol him for GCSEs in the future.

Colin has been in the new prison 2 months. He says he is 'repeating stuff' in English when he needs to be learning about Shakespeare in order to help him with his GCSEs. He enjoys his lessons but feels that the teachers in the prison have low expectations of the pupils. He told us: 'I've learnt nothing much. Everything is taught too basic, below my level. The subjects should go up to higher levels. People could do higher level work if pushed to do so but we're just given low quality work.'

Colin says he was given no choice of subjects in education. He wants to study science and business studies but the prison does not offer these subjects. Colin wants to move back to his previous prison so he can take his GCSEs. When Colin is released from prison he would like to go to college and have a career in computing.

Young offenders' institutions failing to educate inmates

Young offenders' institutions are failing to provide inmates with adequate education and training, the chief inspector of prisons said today.

According to Anne Owers, young offenders are taught by inexperienced staff and offered little vocational training, thus ensuring the institutions fall 'far from meeting' their targets.

The report by the prisons inspectorate, *A Second Chance*, was published today alongside a detailed plan to improve education and training by the Youth Justice Board.

The board's plan said little was being done to improve levels of literacy and numeracy for the 3,000 youngsters in the care of the prison service and proposed £40m of investment to improve standards.

Ms Owers said the inspectorate's account was a 'progress report' into detention and training orders one year after they were introduced as part of the youth justice system.

'It describes a system which is clearly still in development and in transition and which is dealing with an extremely demanding and vulnerable group of young people,' she said, adding, 'We hope that its conclusions will assist the positive development of the system, to support the staff and young people within it.'

Among the key findings was that effective teaching was difficult because of the constantly changing prison population, staff shortages, unpredictable attendance patterns and varying degrees of motivation.

Few teachers had experience of working in secondary or special schools and the provision of vocational training was generally lacking.

Arrangements for girls had suffered because of the uncertainty surrounding the role the prison service had in providing for them, the report said.

The report also found some examples of good practice but in general claimed the quality and provision of education and training for young people was inadequate, especially for female and remand prisoners.

The report recommended a greater use of creative educational methods, better training and support for teachers as well as integrating education and training as a central part of each institution's regime.

'Young offenders are taught by inexperienced staff and offered little vocational training'

Using the information in the report, the Youth Justice Board today launched plans aimed at significantly improving education and training.

The board announced that it had agreed a plan with the Home Office to invest £40m over a three-year period to achieve the target of providing a minimum of 30 hours a week of education and training.

Lord Warner, chairman of the Youth Justice Board, said: 'This report indicates that the scale of literacy and numeracy deficits among young offenders is even worse than had been anticipated and highlights the huge task that education providers have to face in providing education to young people sentenced to custody.'

The board's findings included the fact that around 50% of youngsters in youth offenders' institutions had the numeracy ability of an average seven-year-old child.

The majority of offenders had not been in full-time education prior to custody, and only one in six discharged into the community as part of their detention and training order had education or training provision immediately on release.

Offences committed

Every year the Youth Justice Board commissions a survey into the thoughts and experiences of the youngsters living in England and Wales today. In the first two months of 2001, MORI quizzed 5,263 schoolchildren aged 11-16 and 500 young people excluded from school but attending educational programmes.

Have you committed any criminal offence in the last 12 months?

Survey 2000	Yes – 22%
Survey 2001	Yes – 25%

In almost every category the percentage of children committing the offence has increased.

What offences have you committed?

	2000	2001
Fare dodging	44%	49%
Damaged or destroyed property	26%	29%
Vandalised property (graffiti)	29%	34%
Shop theft	31%	35%
Stolen from school	15%	23%
Stolen from home or where you live	14%	19%
Taken a bicycle without permission	7%	6%
Broken into a building to steal	7%	7%
Bought, held or sold stolen property	19%	25%
Physically assaulted someone	24%	31%
Threatened someone	15%	18%

Source: Youth Justice Board News, March 2001

Youth justice

How changes in the law might affect you

If you don't break the law, the information in this article probably won't affect you. But if you DO, you will find that the police deal with young offenders in a different way now because the law has changed.

So, if you do break the law – even once, and even by committing a so-called minor offence – you will find yourself involved in criminal proceedings that could easily end up with you going to court and getting a criminal conviction. This is because there are now limits on how many 'last chances' the police can give you before you end up in court.

The Crime and Disorder Act 1998 is the law that has changed the system for dealing with young offenders.*

If you commit a really serious offence you will be prosecuted straight away.

If you commit a less serious offence, the police can give you a maximum of only two chances before you will definitely be taken to court. * Young offenders are defined as those aged from 10 to 17 (that is up to, but not including, their 18th birthday) who have broken the law.

Why does being taken to court matter?

If you are taken to court and found guilty of an offence, you will be sentenced and convicted as a criminal. This criminal conviction can then ruin opportunities for you in the future.

A criminal conviction could mean:
* employers refusing to give you a job;
* being refused travel visas, so you would not be allowed to visit some countries;
* being refused insurance for your home or car, or having to pay more for insurance.

Remember – if you are a convicted criminal your police record may last all your life.

How has the law changed?

Before the new law came in, a young offender could get lots of police cautions before being sent to court. This can't happen any more. Now, if you break the law, the police give you a Reprimand. If you break the law again, you will get a Warning. If you then break the law a further time, the police will send you to court. You could say it's now 'two strikes and you're out'. So once you commit any crime, however 'small', you enter the criminal justice system and are in serious trouble. And if the first offence is not for a 'minor' crime then you will be in even more trouble.

1. The first time you break the law:
If it is not a serious offence, you are given a Reprimand. If the offence is more serious, you get a Warning. For a very serious first offence, you get sent straight to court and are prosecuted.

2. The second time you break the law:
If it is not a serious offence, you are given a Warning. For a serious second offence, or if you have already been given a Warning in the last two years, you will go straight to court and be prosecuted.

3. If you break the law for a third time, whatever the offence, even a minor one, you will automatically be sent to court and be prosecuted.

What is a Reprimand?

If you are given a Reprimand, the police officer talks to you about what you have done and explains what will happen to you if you break the law again. They will remind you about who you have hurt by breaking the law – your family as well as your victim. The police will keep a record of your crime. You may find that your details are passed on to a Youth Offending Team who will decide if any further action should be taken.

What is a Warning?

If you are given a Warning, the police talk to you and put your crimes on record in the same way as for a Reprimand. You are automatically referred to a Youth Offending Team who will generally decide what type of scheme to put you on to stop you committing any more crimes. This is your last chance to stop breaking the law and the Youth Offending Team will try to help you.

What is prosecution?

Prosecution means your case will be heard in the Youth Court. If the

Court finds you guilty, you will be sentenced. You will then have a criminal conviction.

Reprimands and Warnings can only be given to people who have admitted that they have broken the law. This means that someone who has committed an offence and does not admit it cannot be given a Reprimand or Warning. In these cases they will be sent to court and prosecuted.

What records are kept of young offenders?

If the police Reprimand you, Warn you, or charge you with a recordable offence, for their records they will take:

- your fingerprints;
- a photograph of you; and
- a hair or saliva sample to record your DNA.

These records, and a written description of you and the offence you committed, will be added to the files on the Police National Computer (PNC). What happens to these records depends on your age at the time and other circumstances, but generally:

- If you are under 16 when you get a Reprimand or Warning the records will stay 'live' until you are 18;
- if you are over 16 when you get a Reprimand, it will be wiped from your records when you are 18 as long as you don't also get a Warning before then;
- if you are over 16 then you get a Warning, the record of the Warning and any Reprimand you have got in the past will stay 'live' for two years from the date of the Warning – even if this goes beyond your 18th birthday;
- but if you go to court, whatever your age, the records of any convictions could be kept on the PNC all your life.

Recordable offences are ones that fall into categories decided by the Government. Most crimes are recordable. Non-recordable offences are generally minor ones like dropping litter and riding a bicycle on the pavement.

If you are convicted in court of a criminal offence, a record of it may be kept for the rest of your life.

Advice and guidance

If you are under 17 years old, you must have someone known as an 'Appropriate Adult' with you. This is to help you understand what is happening while the police investigate the offence. This should be your parent, carer or a member of an Appropriate Adult Scheme or a social worker.

You can also get free legal advice from a solicitor.

Remember if you break the law you will be given a maximum of only two chances – one Reprimand and one Warning before being sent to court. If you commit a serious offence, you won't be given any chances at all, but will be taken straight to court and be prosecuted. This may lead to a criminal conviction.

- The above information is produced by the Metropolitan Police Youth Justice Task Force.

Woolf's ruling could put more children in jail

Lord Woolf's new guidelines to the courts issued yesterday could lead to a substantial increase in the length of custodial sentences handed down to children. Half of all mobile phone robberies are committed by boys aged 16 and under.

There has been a massive rise in mobile phone robberies, distorting the figures for street crime, especially in London.

Recent figures showed that muggers in the capital were snatching phones at a rate of almost 3,000 every month – a fivefold increase in two years. The chance of being a victim is greatest for those aged 11 to 16 and many phones are stolen from children on their way home from school by other pupils.

Half of the victims are children and the peak age for the robbers is 16, with 70 per cent of them under 18.

Five per cent of younger teenagers say they have had a phone stolen at least once. For those under 16 in deprived city areas, the figure rises to 12 per cent.

Research suggests that the sharp rise in phone thefts is fuelling an alarming rise in street robbery, while other types of crime are going down.

A recent study based on surveys in seven police areas showed that the most likely phone robber is male, younger than most other kinds of robbers – with most aged only 14 to 17 – most probably black and operating in a gang.

Fewer than 10 per cent of phone thefts are carried out by teenage girls.

Lord Woolf's proposed tougher sentences will be welcomed by many who believe that the threat of prison is a deterrent to criminals.

However, his comments are surprising given his reputation among penal reformers as a liberal who does not believe in the 'prison works' philosophy.

Last year he said he would prefer to see jails closed rather than new ones opened. He also urged judges to reduce the use of custody 'to what is the acceptable and appropriate minimum'.

He added: 'A short custodial sentence is a very poor alternative to a sentence to be served in the community.'

Lord Woolf's ruling means a minimum jail sentence of 18 months will apply irrespective of the robber's age or whether they are first offenders.

Since young men are responsible for most robberies, this is likely to mean a sharp increase both in the number being sent to jail and the length of time they serve.

About 2,000 children under 17 are held in Young Offender Institutions and make up less than four per cent of the total prison population.

The average sentence for young male offenders is 11 months.

Serious crime by the young doubles in 7 years

The number of young people committing serious crimes, including murder and grievous bodily harm, has almost doubled in seven years.

Home Office figures to be released tomorrow will show that 561 youngsters aged from 10 to 17 committed what are called 'grave crimes' in 2000, up from 315 in 1993.

The figures show that the number of children found guilty of serious offences has surged in the past 30 years. In 1970, six young people were found guilty of grave crimes, 39 in 1975 and 154 in 1985. By 2000, the last year for which statistics are available, there had been a 78-per-cent increase in seven years.

Tom Watson, a Labour member of the Commons home affairs select committee, said: 'We are all aware that far too many young people get involved in crime.

'It's quite terrifying to realise the number of youngsters sentenced at Crown court has doubled in just seven years. The Government is trying to reduce crime, with some success, but this is a problem for society as a whole.

'We need to step back and think why would a 14-year-old mug an old lady or why a 12-year-old would carry a knife, because if we don't stop this now the consequences for the future are disturbing.'

The new figures will alarm many who are worried about youngsters becoming involved in serious crimes. Recent years have seen a series of terrible crimes involving children and youngsters. Two weeks ago a gang of youths aged 14-15 chased, and then raped, a girl in Guildford shopping centre, in Surrey, on a Saturday afternoon.

In May last year, a 16-year-old and 17-year-old were found guilty of torturing a 39-year-old man to death in Stockport near Manchester in a horrific and prolonged attack.

Many youths have also become involved in violent gang warfare in

recent years. On Friday 40 boys robbed other children who were leaving a cinema in London of their mobile phones.

> ### The courts increasingly view muggings and burglaries as serious crimes and also many young people have become involved in such activities to fund drug habits

---

The figures will be released in a report called *Children who Commit Grave Crimes* from Nacro, the crime reduction charity which helps to rehabilitate offenders.

They have been compiled from Home Office records by Tim Bate-

man, of Nacro, who wrote the report. He said that there were several reasons for the increase in serious youth crimes.

The courts increasingly view muggings and burglaries as serious crimes and also many young people have become involved in such activities to fund drug habits.

The statistics show that the vast majority of the increase is because more young people are committing serious violent crime, such as muggings.

The number of murders carried out by 10- to 17-year-olds has not increased significantly but the numbers of violent robberies and persistent burglaries have all increased.

In 1995, for instance, 67 young people were sentenced at Crown court for violence against the person, rising to 108 in 2000. Over the same period, the number of youngsters sentenced for drug offences rose from five to 32. The greatest rise was in robbery, up from 192 in 1995 to 268 in 2000.

A crime committed by a young person is classified as grave if an adult could receive 14 years or more in prison for the same offence. Included are murder, manslaughter, wounding with intent and causing grievous bodily harm.

In such cases, the Youth Court, which can only give a maximum of two years in prison for a crime, declines to hear the case and instead sends the young person to stand trial at a Crown court – where they can receive an adult sentence up to and including life.

In its report, Nacro will suggest setting up a new kind of youth court with extended powers to sentence and supervise young criminals to ensure they do not re-offend.

• By David Bamber, Home Affairs Correspondent

Living safely

Personal safety in your daily life

We all want to live free and active lives; to feel safe and secure wherever we are; at home and out and about.

However, we cannot deny that we seem to be living in a more aggressive society and many of us fear being the victim of a personal assault.

In fact, despite the lurid headlines, the average person's chances of physical attack from a stranger are very low. It is important to remember that most assaults are on men by men. Also, taking care of your personal safety does not mean that you have to shut yourself away in a fortress.

This information will help you to lead life to the full so that you are not constrained by those fears and anxieties. If you plan ahead and practise the suggested skills and strategies, you will reduce the risks and be able to react instinctively and with confidence, should you ever find yourself in a difficult situation.

P.L.A.N. your own personal safety campaign

Prepare yourself
- Assess your risks. We can all take responsibility for our own personal safety, taking steps to modify or change our behaviour according to the risks.
- Try to be relaxed. You can escalate an aggressive situation if you are rushed, stressed or afraid.
- Avoid confrontation. Do not meet aggression with aggression. Talk your way out of problems: stay calm, speak gently, slowly and clearly. Breathe out slowly to help you relax.
- Respect other people's space. Each of us has our personal buffer zone which we are quick to defend.
- Avoid an aggressive stance: crossed arms, hands on hips, a

The Suzy Lamplugh Trust
The Leading Authority on Personal Safety
Registered Charity No. 802567
www.suzylamplugh.org

wagging finger or raised arm will challenge and confront. Avoid looking down on anyone or touching someone unnecessarily.

Look confident
A confident person is much less likely to be attacked.
- Be alert when out and about. Walk tall.
- Keep fit. Good posture, stamina, strength and tension control can all aid personal safety.
- Hold your head up, be aware of your surroundings and the potential hazards.
- Know where you are going and how to get there.

Avoid putting yourself at risk
Your aim is to stay safe!
- Thinking things through and planning for the unexpected helps you to feel confident and react well in an emergency.
- Read this article often. 'If this were to happen – then what would I do?' Take a few moments to consider what you would do if a problem should occur.
- Let someone know, or at least a note to say where you are going and when you will be back. If your plans change tell someone.

Never assume
- . . . it won't happen to me. Nobody is invincible. Even though the chances are slight, don't bury your head in the sand.
- . . . your fears are unfounded. Do not ignore your instincts or that 'funny feeling'. ACT straight away.
- . . . people are what they seem. Appearances can be deceptive.
- . . . that your mobile phone will work.

Physical attack
If you do meet a problem, your primary aim should be to get away.
- Walk away as fast as you can. Head for a place where you know there are people.
- Don't look back. Try not to panic. Blow out so you can breathe properly and reduce tension.
- Yell or shout 'Phone the police' or another instruction to which people respond quickly.
- Use a personal attack alarm to shock and disorientate an assailant. This will gain vital seconds for you to get away.
- Report any incident as soon as possible. You may save someone else.
- Physical self-defence should only be a last resort. It limits your options and commits you to a fight you could lose. It is not weak to walk away from violence.
- If you see someone else in danger – ring 999 – ask for the police and give a clear message with a location.

Safe at home
We naturally feel safer at home but there are still things we should do.

Callers you do not know
- Fit a door chain and spyhole; outside lighting lets you identity callers.

- Before opening the door, put on the door chain and ask for proof of identity. Keep them waiting until you are satisfied, even if it's a woman or a child.
- Public service employees are required to show an identity card. Examine it carefully as fake cards can be used. The card should include a photograph of the holder and the name of the organisation. Don't be taken in by someone who says they have left their card behind.
- If you're at all suspicious, phone the organisation concerned to check, and the police if necessary. Don't worry if it turns out to be a false alarm.
- If you're selling your home, try not to show people around on your own. Tell your estate agent to send a representative with prospective buyers, or ask a friend or neighbour to be there with you.

Nuisance phone calls and harassment

- Obscene and indecent phone calls are a criminal offence. You do not have to talk to anyone unless you want to. As soon as you realise you are receiving a nuisance or obscene call, hang up gently with no emotion. Most random callers are put off if they do not receive a reaction. If the calls, including silent ones, persist report them to the police. You can also trace a call by dialling 1471.
- If you are being stalked or harassed, check the Suzy Lamplugh Trust web site for information, or send in a stamped self-addressed envelope (41p) to the Trust. You can also call the Victim Support Helpline on 0845 30 30 900.

Personal possessions

Out and about

- Ideally, carry essential valuables such as a wallet in a secure outside pocket.
- Use a money belt.
- Keep your cheque book separate from your cheque card.
- Keep these items in a pocket: a note of 24-hour numbers to

cancel your cards; small change; travel pass.
- In public places keep your bag or briefcase on your lap. If you have to, put it on the floor – preferably between your legs – and secure the strap.
- Don't leave coats and jackets containing valuables unattended.

In your car

- Keep anything of value such as bags or mobile phones out of view – they make easy pickings for a snatch thief in stop-go traffic, especially if left on the front passenger seat. Keep your doors locked.
- Don't leave valuables in a parked car. Never leave your car unlocked, even on a garage forecourt when you go to pay for petrol.

At work

- The workplace is a popular target for casual thieves. Keep your bag and other personal belongings locked in a cupboard and drawer.

Use your card wisely

- Sign any cards as soon as they arrive. Ensure you cut up the old cards immediately the new ones become valid.
- Don't write your PIN number down or give it to anyone – even bank staff.
- When using your plastic card, ask for the carbon paper from the transaction.

- Keep transaction slips to check against your statement.
- Avoid using cash points in badly lit or isolated areas, particularly late at night.
- It only takes a moment to report lost or stolen cards to your bank or building society – so make sure you do as soon as possible.

Walking

People tend to feel more vulnerable when walking, especially after dark. You can prepare yourself to recognise and avoid potential dangers.

- Dress appropriately and wear clothes and shoes that are easy to move in.
- Try to keep at least one hand free. Laden down with bags, you're less mobile.
- Use your senses and be aware of your surroundings. Wearing a personal stereo will dull your hearing.
- Try to keep to well-lit streets and walk facing oncoming traffic.
- Avoid danger spots such as poorly lit subways, car parks, deserted buildings, waste ground or alleyways.
- Don't be tempted to take short cuts through potential danger spots, even if you're in a hurry.
- Be on your guard with strangers; avoid crowds or groups which may feel threatening; be wary of parked vehicles with the engine running and people sitting in them.

If problems arise

GET AWAY. Walking fast is usually safer than trying to run. If you think someone is following you, check by crossing and re-crossing the street. If they persist, move quickly to the nearest place with people and call the police.

If a vehicle stops next to you and you are threatened, turn and move quickly in the opposite direction. You can turn faster than a car. Make for the nearest public place and phone the police.

Cycling

Cycling can be one of the safest means of travel. Be as prepared as you can.

- Keep your bike in good working order: check lights, brakes and tyres regularly.
- Dress to be seen and safe: helmet; luminous strips; toe clips. Make sure you can hear.
- Have a loud piercing horn and mirrors.
- Look purposeful and competent. If a route is new to you, plan it before you leave home.
- Avoid short cuts even if you're in a hurry.
- Keep moving if someone signals for help. Wave to show you have registered the problem and go on to the next convenient phone.

Public transport

Travelling by public transport is generally very safe, but simple precautions can reduce risk and give you greater confidence.

- Know where you are going and which stop you need. Check departure times, especially of last buses and trains.
- Have your ticket or change ready.
- Try to walk near other people who do not appear to present a risk, and walk purposefully to your destination.
- Carry some money, and the number of a reliable taxi company.
- Make sure you know where help points, or an alarm, are located, so that you know where they are should an emergency arise.

Buses

- When waiting, stand in a well-lit place near groups of people.
- If the bus is empty, or it's dark, sit on the lower deck, near the driver.

Trains

- Wait where it is well lit and there are other people.
- Stand well back on the platform.
- Avoid compartments which have no access to corridors or other parts of the train.
- It is safer to sit with other people and avoid empty carriages.

- If you feel you may be at risk, move to another seat or carriage. You can get off at the next stop, but assess whether you would be safer at that station or on the train: if it is deserted, unmanned station, you will be safer on the train, particularly if you don't know if or where any easily accessible help points or telephones might be located on the station.

If problems arise

Of you feel threatened or there is an incident, act immediately.

- Alert the driver, guard or conductor by making as much noise as possible.
- Pull the emergency alarm.
- Look for station staff, British Transport Police or a Help Point if there's an incident on the platform.

- The above information is an extract from, *Living Safely – Personal Safety in your Daily Life*, a leaflet produced by the Suzy Lamplugh Trust. They also publish *World Wise – Your Passport to Safer Travel*, a guide to safer travel abroad for independent travellers, the directory is regularly updated on the internet at www.suzylamplugh.org/worldwise. They also sell a personal shriek alarm, £7.50 plus p&p. See page 41 for details on how to contact them.

© The Suzy Lamplugh Trust

Tackling street crime

Met takes drastic action to tackle street crime

More police officers are being assigned to combat street crime to boost the Met's campaign for safer streets while continuing the substantial operation to protect London against terrorism

Announcing the measures Commissioner Sir John Stevens explained:

'Tackling street crime and maintaining security are imperatives for the Met. Both have generated significant demands on us since September 11th and we need to build on our efforts to protect London and Londoners from these threats. To continue to fulfil our policing

- 315 traffic officers available for anti-streetcrime work
- 160 traffic wardens switched to high visibility patrols
- 100 Territorial Support Group officers targeting street crime
- Targeting of 320 persistent young offenders
- Eight boroughs designated for special anti-streetcrime operations

responsibilities in these two important areas now demands radical short-term action which will have an impact on other policing needs in London.'

In broad terms the plan will result in 475 officers being redirected to tackle street crime in the boroughs whilst security patrols in central London and strategic sites are maintained.

To achieve this 315 traffic officers will be redeployed and/or made available to the boroughs and 160 traffic wardens will be switched to high visibility and security patrols. In addition to this 100 Territorial Support Group officers will be used to target street crime in central London whilst continuing to remain available to deal with emergency situations.

The new measures are being introduced over a period of two weeks and will be reviewed at the end of March.

Targeting persistent offenders

Simultaneously borough commands are being tasked to target the 320 persistent young offenders identified across London who are believed to be responsible for a disproportionate level of street crime.

Eight boroughs in particular will be designated for street robbery operations involving specialist units similar to the Met's recent Operation Strongbox. These are:
- Westminster
- Lambeth
- Hackney
- Southwark
- Camden
- Tower Hamlets
- Haringey
- Brent

Extra patrols will assist police

The use of traffic wardens on security patrols is a precursor of the Met's plan to recruit and deploy several hundred police auxiliaries later this year to provide 'eyes and ears' for security and intelligence gathering whilst freeing up officers to concentrate on crime fighting in the boroughs.

The Commissioner admits that hard choices have had to be made in relation to the redeployment of traffic officers and wardens although motorway patrols and fatal accident investigations will not be affected.

Action required from others too

The Commissioner has also warned that the Met alone will not be able to make a significant impact on street robbery without commitment and action from other agencies. Secure accommodation in the capital is limited and street robbery has risen despite a 26.6 per cent increase in arrests made by police this year.

'To put it bluntly there will not be much gained if the Met continues to arrest more street robbers who are then simply processed and freed to rob again – so-called "revolving door justice",' said the Commissioner.

To counter this the Met wants the Government to consider sentencing for robbery emulating the successful 'three strikes and you're out' policy for burglary. It is also seeking tighter bail restrictions for street robbers.

Mobile phones and youth crime

The Met has already run several initiatives aimed at tackling the particular problem posed by mobile phone thefts and the Commissioner made it clear that this remains a priority.

- 26.6% increase in arrests
- But robbers freed to rob again
- '3 strikes and you're out' sentencing policy should be considered
- Mobile phones account for between a half and a third of street robberies

'We now have mobile phones accounting for between a third and half of street robberies in London and it is time for the mobile phone industry to introduce some effective crime prevention measures which would disable stolen phones and make them less attractive to steal,' he said.

The Met has been at the forefront of addressing youth crime through partnership with local authorities, schools and other agencies but much more remains to be done. Next week sees the launch of a pilot scheme in two boroughs for a new Crimestoppers scheme for young people and the Met will be joining forces with the Youth Justice Board to host a youth crime conference later this year.

The Commissioner concluded: 'We are committed to tackling this problem at both ends. At one end we are working with others to identify potential young offenders and divert them before they are embedded in a life of crime; at the other end we are deploying hard-edged policing to deal with persistent and violent street robbers.

'What we also need is a criminal justice system that is robust enough to deliver the safety and security that Londoners deserve.'

• The above information is from the Metropolitan Police Service's web site which can be found at www.met.police.uk Alternatively, see page 41 for their address details.
© Metropolitan Police Service

Children and crime reduction

Victims not villains. Jackie Hall examines the demonisation of children in crime reduction strategies

There are almost no official statistics on the scale of child victimisation. The *British Crime Survey* does not talk to under 16-year-olds and official crime statistics only look at children's victimisation in relation to crimes where age is a factor, which is mainly sex offences. However, we do know from research, notably from the University of Durham and Nottinghamshire Police, that children and young people are more likely to be victims of high volume crimes such as theft from the person, assault, harassment from adults and peers and serious bullying and the National Association for the Care and Rehabilitation of Offenders has estimated that one in three children aged 12 to 15 are assaulted every year. Research conducted by Nottinghamshire Police shows that 95% of crimes committed against children and young people are not reported.

The NSPCC is extremely concerned that local authorities are not paying sufficient attention to the needs of young people who experience crime. It recently analysed a sample of local authority crime reduction strategies for 1999-2002 and was dismayed to find that fewer than half referred to victim support for children and young people or to child protection issues and only 11% were committed to tackling children's fear of crime. In Nottinghamshire's strategy, for example, only 147 young people were consulted out of a population of over 250,000 young people, despite the fact that crime against children and young people had risen by over 10%.

Children and young people are not being completely ignored in the crime reduction agenda. In fact they are cast right at the heart as the chief cause of problems, appearing in most strategies as potential or actual offenders, the cause of fear and disorder, as drug takers and as members of society who just hang around causing trouble.

The vast majority of young people are law-abiding members of communities and yet they tell us stories about being reported to the police and moved on, simply for being in a group of three or more in a public place. Would we accept this as adults? The expansion of curfews for young people highlights government's concentration on children and young people as potential trouble-makers and is an infringement of their right to use their community. Some may say they are used for the safety of the children but we don't tell adults to all go home because they

---

Children and young people are the group most likely to be victimised by crime and their needs should be prioritised as such in all crime reduction strategies

---

might get assaulted – we put measures in place to avoid it happening (for example CCTV outside pubs and clubs) and a system that takes the issue seriously when it does.

A community assessment carried out by the NSPCC found adults fearful of young people hanging around outside the local Spar but young people told us they like to be there because it is well lit and people are around, so they feel safe. A number of Crime and Disorder strategies that did talk to young people confirm the fact that young people hang around in groups primarily for their own safety, not to intimidate.

According to Sergeant Dave Padley who carried out the Nottinghamshire research, 'we have got to stop demonising young people and have got to start respecting them first and foremost as members of our communities and society, but particularly as more vulnerable members'. They have as much right as adults to be kept safe, to be able to contact the police without feeling their issues will be trivialised, to be able to socialise and go about their business without being moved on, reported, curfewed or, at best, shunned.

Children and young people are the group most likely to be victimised by crime and their needs should be prioritised as such in all crime reduction strategies. They can be a valuable resource in the search for solutions to crime and their involvement and participation is vital if we are going to reduce crime and make neighbourhoods safer.

• Jackie Hall is national co-ordinator of child community safety for the NSPCC. The above information is from *HLM – The Howard League Magazine*, produced by the Howard League for Penal Reform. See page 41 for their address details.

Young victims count too

If only police and politicians took the mugging of teenagers as seriously as the car-jacking of Mercedes

By Ros Coward

Official responses to the recent well-publicised car-jackings speak volumes about who and what this society is prepared to protect. Scotland Yard has now been given the go-ahead to deploy 11 'elite armed response vehicles', manned by marksmen wearing protective clothing and armed with rifles and handguns.

This, apparently, is 'a proportional level' of force against the threat of car-jacking. By contrast, the huge number of muggings currently carried out against 14- to 16-year-olds are not even recorded in the violent crime statistics and, until very recently, had barely registered on the political radar.

Recent reports of car-jacking are horrific, but it is impossible not to conclude that property theft and threat to middle-class people is taken much more seriously than attacks on those with less status. Currently there are only 1,200 car-jackings a year in London. By contrast there are over 200,000 violent muggings, most involving teenage victims.

But until his recent call for tougher sentencing of mobile phone muggers, the home secretary seemed more concerned to deny this violent crime is increasing, exploiting the exclusion of under-16s from these statistics even though a quarter of all mugging victims are boys between 14 and 17. Trivialising muggings of teenagers is widespread. Police say mobile phone theft is the modern-day equivalent of pocket money theft. Others describe teen-on-teen crime as a rite of passage. I've even heard someone describe teenagers from wealthier backgrounds as fair game, a walking 'resource'.

Tell that to the kids involved. I live in a crime hot spot – Lambeth in London – and while I wouldn't go as far as to say mugging is a daily occurrence, it is an uncomfortably frequent part of my teenage children's universe. Every local teenager has had bikes, money and mobile phones stolen, sometimes just with threats, sometimes with knives and violence.

On one occasion, my son had his face badly bruised. Teenagers won't report these incidents, even though they are often shaken, physically hurt and thoroughly humiliated. They regard the police as useless and on the evidence of the occasions I have dealt with them over such crimes, they are right. One helpfully told me: 'We've lost the plot in this area.'

For most politicians, figures about street robberies involving teenagers are statistical abstractions. Solutions are equally lacking in empathy. It's a matter of improving phone design, or handing out exemplary sentences to regular offenders. Blunkett's stupidest idea has been to transfer police from traffic infringements to street patrolling. Stupid because it so happens teenagers are the main victims of dangerous driving accidents – and deceitful. In my hot spot, there's been no trace of increased police activity.

Anyway, police numbers and length of sentences don't address the cause. The soaring muggings rate is being driven by teenagers attacking other teenagers, rather than being the effect of criminal gangs. The real change is in 'offender behaviour'. Certainly, there are teenage muggers profiting from organised crime but there is also far more opportunistic crime, bullying that shades into theft and violence. My daughter was with friends chatting for some time to another group before having her phone forced off her, fortunately without violence. But this opportunism can be lethal if weapons or extreme violence are used.

Inner-city teenagers are living in a complex and volatile world where psychological issues of race, sexual identity and physical dominance are critical in how chance encounters turn out. Mood, and mood affected by drugs, also play a part. There is no hard-and-fast line between criminals and victims. They often come from the same area, inhabit the same world, may even have started out at the same primary school.

There are similarities with age-old bullying, but now there is more danger, more deliberate humiliation. Classically, an older group of boys picks on a younger one, often of a different race. It's a world where might is right and gang culture reluctantly admired. Police do nothing. Kids keep on the right side of friends who know the 'bad guys' and admire parents who threaten back. Few schools seem remotely up to speed on these issues, still pushing soft and outmoded anti-bullying programmes.

This is a very different teenage world from the one shown on *Pop Idol*. No wonder middle-class parents went so mad about that show. It was the teenage world they wanted to see, not exactly unrealistic but very partial. These kids are the products of music lessons, drama clubs, of aspiring parents cultivating talent and ambition. In *Pop Idol*, peer group rivalry is sublimated to mutual solidarity. It's an idealised world. The reality is so much more complex, a world where teenagers have their freedoms curtailed by threats and their confidence undermined by violence.

Few in power are even describing this world, let alone producing solutions. This is a worrying situation. What will this teenage generation think of politicians who send in armoured teams to defend a Mercedes but who do nothing to make their streets safe?

Mobile muggings highlight a wider problem

The real concern is why society is incapable of dealing with juvenile crime

Metropolitan Police claims last week, that soaring street robbery could be blamed on the need for increased security patrols since September 11, do not stand scrutiny.

Although offences more than doubled in the year to December 2001, the figures are consistent with a long-established increase in this type of crime.

In the first six months of 2001, street robberies in the capital rose by over 20%, to some 5,500 offences in July. The average monthly figure of 6,400 after the US attacks shows therefore a similar rate of increase.

Claims that robbery has been fuelled by mobile phone ownership are more justified, with more than 28% of offences now involving a mobile phone. This, however, does not in itself explain why robberies are increasing.

According to the Home Office, street robberies have increased nationally by 13% over the last two years. Had robberies where only phones were stolen been excluded, the figure would have been 8%. The increase in street robbery cannot, therefore, be blamed entirely on mobile phones.

Even were this to be the case, it would not excuse the apparent inability of the criminal justice system to combat such offending.

Another oft-heard 'explanation' is that much of street crime is 'kids robbing kids', and, by implication, somehow of less consequence. In a society where violent crime is normally regarded as more serious when against children, this apparent reversal of logic in the case of street robbery seems bizarre.

Nor should it be forgotten that a number of people each year actually die in such incidents – a figure likely to rise with an increased use of

By Charles Shoebridge

firearms, such as the shooting of a female victim in London on New Year's Day.

> **Claims that robbery has been fuelled by mobile phone ownership are more justified, with more than 28% of offences now involving a mobile phone**

Asking what is to be done about street robbery is, of course, easier than providing useful answers.

As with all issues, the extent and nature of the problem need first

to be ascertained. In this, the Home Office has taken an important step with the publication today of a report entitled *Mobile Phone Theft*.

It makes grim reading, but contains no surprises for those involved in combating street robbery. Police officers often ask why those researching crime so rarely seem to consult officers or the offenders themselves, rather than academic theorists. This paper makes no such mistake.

Street robbery, as with other crime, can only be tackled successfully with a multi-level approach, not all of which is within the power of the police to deliver.

Thus, for many years it has been known that one of the main problems in tackling phone theft has been the ease with which a stolen handset can be re-used. In theory, each set has a unique electronic identification – the IMEI number.

A service provider can block a handset from being used, once notified of its theft. The IMEI number does not have to be known by the loser, as it can be obtained from the victim's ordinary mobile number. Once blocked, a mobile phone cannot function, regardless of the SIM card used.

Unfortunately, it is a simple matter to alter the electronic identity of a phone. Service providers also state that manufacturers may give more than one phone the same IMEI number – meaning that to block a stolen phone could inconvenience several customers.

These are issues that only the industry can resolve, but Vodafone point out that even the facilities it offers to track stolen mobiles are under-used by police.

Nevertheless, the suspicion remains that, as was once feared the case with car stereos, manufacturers are reluctant to lose the repeat purchases that enhanced security would clearly curtail.

It is often suggested that thefts of mobiles occur because the victim has what the thief does not. Experience suggests otherwise. Much phone theft is a highly organised business, with the robbers giving the sets to handlers who, after any necessary modifications, sell them on wholesale, often for export.

Targeting such handlers is hard work and resource intensive, with convictions difficult to secure. But a successful operation to remove a prominent handler, while not producing numerous clear-ups, will often have a marked effect in reducing crime.

Of course, removing a handler is not the same as convicting him. Courts have a vital role to play in ensuring that handling stolen goods carries more risk of a greater sentence than pure theft, as sentencing guidelines suggest.

The courts also have a role in passing sentences against robbers to protect the community at large.

The Home Office paper faces up to the thorny question of who is committing street robberies, and why. It identifies that, in most areas, young black males are over-whelmingly responsible.

Without acknowledging this – so difficult for the police – very little progress can be made in tackling street crime and its causes. In London, 71% of those charged with such offences are black, although only 8% of London's population is black.

It is not enough to say that poverty alone is a reason for such criminality. The boys who steal do not, generally, have any more materially difficult lives than those on the same estates who do not. Experience suggests, however, that many are excluded from school, and even more are missing a positive male role model.

In resolving street robbery, there are factors at work beyond the ability of the police alone to control. The issue is complex, and separate from that of mobile phones. It involves uncomfortable truths of victimised society in terms of both victim and perpetrator.

Regardless of those complex-ities, the inexorable rise of street robbery marks the apparent inability of society and, in particular, the criminal justice system, to adequately deal with juvenile violent crime. This, rather than the technical properties of phones, is the key issue to be addressed.

• Charles Shoebridge was a serving Metropolitan police officer from 1988 to 2000.

Lokit, Mrkit, KEPit, Usit, DntL0sit!

(or Lock it, Mark it, Keep it, Use it, Don't lose it! for those less familiar with the language of 'texting')

That's the message from the Metropolitan Police Service in a mobile phone crime prevention campaign. It is aimed particularly at school-children but the advice applies equally to phone users of any age.

Eye-catching posters using mobile phone text language have been distributed in London's schools to encourage youngsters to be more cautious when using their mobile phones.

Schools liaison officers are going into all secondary schools to property mark phones and to offer advice on how pupils can prevent their phones being used if they are stolen.

Precautions to take

- Record your phone's IMEI number – which is unique to each phone. If the phone is stolen, this number can then be used by police to prove that the phone is stolen and to return it to the rightful owner.
- The IMEI number is displayed by pressing * # 0 6 # ('star', 'hash', 'zero', 'six', 'hash').
- Get your phone property marked.
- Keep your phone out of sight when you are in public places such as when you are walking in the street.
- Use any security features that are built in to your phone, such as additional security codes.
- If you are not using your phone then keep it turned off.
- If your phone is lost or stolen then report it immediately.

The policing perspective

The campaign has been launched in response to a continued rise in mobile phone thefts. Crime statistics show that in London:

- In half of all street robberies, a mobile phone is stolen
- In two-thirds of those robberies, a mobile phone is the only item taken.
- Fourteen- to 17-year-olds are the age group most likely to be victims of street crime.

Speaking at the campaign launch Supt. Archie Torrance of Westminster Police said:

'The Metropolitan Police take street robbery very seriously and in the past year we have arrested 20% more street robbers compared to the year before. We continue to work to combine high visibility policing with covert operations so we can bring criminals to justice.'

Further information

- For further information about having your mobile phone security marked you can contact the Crime Reduction Office at your local police station.
- Additional advice on protecting your mobile can be found on our crime prevention pages.

• The above information is from the Metropolitan Police's web site which can be found at www.met.police.uk

Young people and Neighbourhood Watch

Young people are particularly vulnerable to certain types of crime and have their own perspective on which crimes matter most. One of the most widespread means of getting involved in crime prevention is by joining or forming a youth group, such as a Youth Action Group, or junior crime prevention panel. These are the young person's version of a crime prevention panel. They are usually attached to a senior panel, or a local school, and deal with areas of crime which are more likely to affect young people. Young people themselves are the driving force of these groups, but they can benefit and take their plans further with help and support from adult groups such as Neighbourhood Watch. And in turn, Neighbourhood Watch schemes get an accurate picture of youth crime in their neighbourhood and can tap into an energetic resource to tackle such problems as:

- alcohol, drugs and substance misuse
- personal safety
- aggression and violence
- car crime
- vandalism and graffiti
- truancy
- bullying
- peer group pressure
- arson
- burglary.

And these are some of the projects they have created to tackle them:

Example one
The Youth Action Group of a girls' school in Swansea decided to tackle the problems centred around the badly run town toilets. Smashed mirrors, broken basins and abusive graffiti all added to a sense of intimidation, and the toilets had become the focal point of bullying so that some younger pupils were too afraid to use them. The Youth Action Group carried out a survey to discover why pupils were afraid, which they presented to the school head and governors. Their action prompted the school to carry out a complete renovation of the building, which has since remained trouble free.

Example two
Pupils in a Stafford school devised a solution to bullying and playground disputes. The head asked every pupil and teacher in the school to identify the person they thought had the good qualities of listening, communication and leadership. The same 20 names kept cropping up, and he trained them in the skills they would need to mediate between disputing groups or individuals. They now staff an office in the school grounds all day, and any pupil with a problem or grievance, or anyone who is being bullied can go to the office for help. They are solving the bullying problem by getting the two sides together to sort it out between them.

For more information on Youth Action Groups in your area contact the Prudential Youth Action Initiative at Crime Concern on 01793 514 596.

Example three
Youth crime prevention doesn't have to be confined to Youth Action Groups. Neighbourhood Watch can also involve young people in their own communities. 17-year-old Samantha Holyman is street co-ordinator for the Pelsall Area Neighbourhood Watch in the West Midlands. She also writes the youth section for the local Neighbourhood Watch Association newsletter. Samantha admits it's the work on the newsletter which attracted her initially, but combined with her work experience in the community safety office of her local police station, it's given her an insight into crime prevention from both the police and civilian side. Samantha also relishes the chance to confront the prejudices some of the older Watch members may have against young people. Involvement with such schemes also introduces young people to networks, where they can learn more ideas and find out about where their activity fits into the broader scheme of things. A recent youth crime event in the Midlands was attended by over 100 teenagers representing schools in the area. Representatives also attended from the police, probation service and the National Association for the Care and Resettlement of Offenders. It's this kind of pooling of ideas and sharing of perspectives which encourages young people that they can contribute something to the fight against crime.

'All this talk of crime makes me anxious. . .'
When you first join Neighbourhood Watch you may be given a lot of information about crime, especially

in your area. This may alarm you. But remember – the risk of actually being a victim of violent crime is very small indeed.

Most crime – more than 90 per cent – is against property, not people, and most of your security measures will be aimed at protecting your home and your belongings. Neighbourhood Watch is all about taking sensible precautions. It reassures vulnerable members of your community that you are keeping a neighbourly eye on them.

How much should I do?
It's entirely up to you. Some people have more free time than others, and may want to take a very active role as a committee member or even co-

ordinator of a local Watch scheme.
- You may know something about marketing or communications, and volunteer to write and distribute newsletters, or publicise your local scheme's activities.
- You may be in business locally and know of avenues to seek sponsorship for Watch activities.
- Or your part may be as simple as keeping a lookout while your neighbour is on holiday, making sure there are no tell-tale signs such as milk left on a doorstep that would attract a burglar.

Everyone can do something that will really make a difference.

How can I set up a scheme?
If you are serious about getting

involved in Neighbourhood Watch you will want to find out about other schemes and how they operate. Your local police will tell you if there is a scheme in your area or help you set up one of your own.

The National Neighbourhood Watch Association can provide information and help. Visit the Association's web site at www.neighbourhoodwatch.net

• For a copy of *Your Practical Guide to Crime Prevention* contact the Crime Prevention Officer at your local police station or write to: Crime Prevention Publicity, Home Office, Room 155, 50 Queen Anne's Gate, London SW1H 9AT.

Lessons from Europe?

John Muncie reflects on differing approaches to tackling youth crime and argues that the UK should no longer follow America's lead

Transatlantic policy transfers in both social and criminal justice matter have become increasingly common. In the past decade, not only welfare-to-work but also zero tolerance policing, boot camps, curfews, electronic monitoring, mandatory minimum sentences, the naming and shaming of young offenders and strict controls over parents have all been transported from the USA to England. In America it is well known that the numbers in prison have increased at an unprecedented rate since the 1980s, a phenomenon criminologists now refer to as 'mass imprisonment, carceral hyper-inflation' and 'hyper-incarceration'. In the youth justice arena there has been widespread dismantling of special court procedures, in place for much of the 20th century, and designed to protect young people from the stigma and formality of adult justice. Since the 1980s most American states have expanded the charges for which juvenile defendants can be tried as adults in criminal courts, lowered the age at which this can be done, changed the purpose of their juvenile codes to prioritise punishment and resorted to more punitive

training and boot camps. In some states there is now no age limit at all to adult criminal prosecution and trial. One Texas legislator has chillingly advocated executing 11-year-olds. In England and Wales such shifts have been mirrored in the abolition of the presumption of *doli incapax* for 10- to 14-year-olds, in the establishment of secure training centres, and in new powers for the Home Secretary to send 10-year-olds to custody. Overt boot camps may have been abandoned but the juvenile penal estate has expanded greatly and the number of young people sentenced to custody in England and Wales has doubled from just 4,000 in 1992 to over 7,500 in 1999.

Channel crossing
The UK countries (and Ireland) have the lowest ages of criminal responsibility in the EU and the most recent comparative data from the Council of Europe (1996) indicates that with the exception of Ireland and Turkey, England and Scotland have the highest percentage of their prison population under the age of 21. None of our European neighbours have moved to such a dramatic

repenalisation of young offending as witnessed in America and England. European comparative research is patchy but a number of potentially decriminalising and decarcerative processes can be noted that place English repenalisation in a particularly stark relief:
- In France, a series of violent disturbances in Lyons and Marseilles in the 1980s were dealt with not by repressive authoritarian measures, but by developing education and vocational opportunities and avenues for local political participation. The Bonnemaison initiative involved the recruitment of older youth to act as paid youth workers with youngsters in the suburbs. These were connected with residents and local government officials to form crime prevention committees designed to address urban redevelopment as well as security issues. It is widely believed that the initiative was at least initially successful in achieving a greater integration particularly for children of North African origin.

A number of other European examples of recent youth justice

reform raise the question of whether England and the USA are in fact atypical in their response to young offending.

- In Holland, youth prison populations were reduced in the 1970s by limiting penal capacity, emphasising rehabilitation and supporting a culture of tolerance. HALT projects begun in Rotterdam in 1981 and various other social crime prevention initiatives appear to have had an impact on vandalism, truancy and shoplifting by replacing judicial intervention with reparation schemes and advice agencies to improve youth's 'survival skills'.

- In Belgium, special youth brigades exist in most police forces, often staffed by officers holding social work diplomas. All judicial interventions are legitimated through an educative, rather than punitive, responsibilising discourse.

- In Italy, judges have an additional power to grant a 'judicial pardon' which together with a policy of 'liberta controllata' (a form of police supervision) means that young people are incarcerated only for a very few serious violent offences.

- In Finland, the number of young people in prison has dropped by 90 per cent since 1960 without any associated rise in known offending. This was achieved by suspending imprisonment on the condition that a period of probation was successfully completed. Immediate 'unconditional' sentencing to custody is now a rarity.

Throughout Europe, various commentators detected an opening up of juvenile justice in the 1990s with the use of custodial sanctions declining. Community safety and restorative initiatives – reparation, community work, courses in social training and so on – together with a much greater compliance with UN rules and Council of Europe recommendations are all directed towards avoiding youth imprisonment. In contrast, the reversion to custody in England and Wales is in direct contradiction to the United Nations

Convention on the Rights of the Child which stipulated that the 'best interests' of the child shall prevail and that youth custody should be a last resort and be used for the shortest possible time. UN monitoring of UK policy has led to conclude that the human rights of British children are not being upheld. Its insistence that secure training centres be abolished and that serious consideration be given to raising the age of criminal responsibility has been consistently ignored. The European Convention on Human Rights also confers the right to respect for private and family life and protects families from arbitrary interference. The new parenting orders, child curfews and anti-social behaviour orders in English youth justice would again appear to be in contempt. Nowhere in Europe, other than in England and Wales and Ireland, can parents be subjected to punitive supervision measures as part of youth justice law.

Critics of this argument will be quick to point out that there have been some innovative developments in youth justice in England and Wales, such as the introduction of referral and reparation orders. These orders, with an emphasis on offender/victim participation and harm minimisation rather than crime control, draw in part upon the

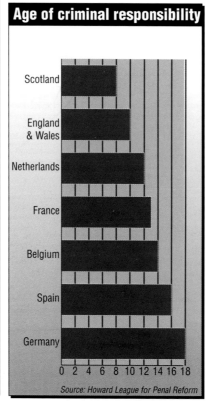

Age of criminal responsibility

Scotland

England & Wales

Netherlands

France

Belgium

Spain

Germany

0 2 4 6 8 10 12 14 16 18

Source: Howard League for Penal Reform

experience of conferencing in Australasia and the children's hearing system in Scotland.

In New Zealand and in six Australian states restorative justice processes are established in statute as the fundamental rationale for youth justice. Formal court processes are by-passed in preference for various types of family group conferences. Most academic research speaks highly of such an approach in impacting on re-offending and on ensuring that both victim and offender are the key decision-makers in determining any future action. Moreover they tend to be used for medium and serious offences and are not siphoned-off merely to deal with the trivial. In contrast in England and Wales restorative principles appear rather more peripheral – as yet another option in an escalating number of possible outcomes. In Australasia professional decision-making and the role of the courts is marginal to an extent not contemplated in England. Much of this is probably due to their greater ideological commitment to policies that emphasise social welfare and community involvement rather than US-style incarceration. In England and Wales early reports of referral orders in pilot are somewhat mixed with the low level of involvement of victims being a particular stumbling block. The tension remains between the inclusionary and participatory aspirations of restorative justice and the exclusionary and net-widening potential of criminality prevention. Moreover in all the current rhetoric of risk, harm, safety and inclusion within 'what works' audits and evaluations, little or no attention seems to be given to young people's own safety or to their own extraordinarily high levels of victimisation.

- John Muncie is a senior lecturer in criminology and social policy at the Open University. The above information is from *HLM – The Howard League Magazine*, produced by the Howard League for Penal Reform. See page 41 for their address details.

Why restorative justice?

Repairing the harm caused by crime. Roger Graef, award-winning film-maker and criminologist, on the principles, practices and effectiveness of restorative justice – based on case studies, an invaluable guide for all justice practitioners

I filmed a mediation dealing with the damage a young boy had caused to a garage owner's precious motorbike. The victim was furious, and initially refused to meet the boy and his family. But the mediator helped the victim to tell the lad how much the bike meant to him, and how angry he was. The boy's father was also ashamed and angry. The boy was dismayed that a prank he had done as a dare had caused such distress. The victim was moved to accept his apology. After the session, he gave the lad a ride on the back of his bike, and promised to teach him motor mechanics.'

In Winnipeg, Canada, some 900 cases a year are first referred to the local voluntary mediation service by the Crown Prosecution Service. The disputants in such cases as fights have an hour to agree an acceptable resolution, and any reparation. This must be accepted as fair by the bench. If the disputants fail to agree, the case comes to trial.

Restorative justice has been heralded as a new concept in dealing with crimes and disputes. The Government has now enshrined mediation and reparation in both the 1998 Crime and Disorder Act and in the 1999 Youth Justice and Criminal Evidence Act, which came into force in 2000. But few people know what restorative justice is or how it works.

Restorative justice means restoring the balance disturbed by crime, and making good the harm caused to those concerned. It involves victim and offender – and, unlike the traditional criminal justice system, it includes, friends, families and communities. It gives space for victims to explore issues they cannot raise in court, and for offenders to take greater responsibility for their actions. Restorative justice is not just about face-to-face mediation. It can include other kinds of making good,

By Roger Graef

from reparation and community service to community mediation of local conflicts.

Restorative justice has been embedded in law in New Zealand for a decade. It is increasingly used in Canada, the USA and Australia. There are many ways in which restorative justice is moving into British institutions. Already recognised in recent criminal and civil legislation, in some places it is becoming well established, in others it is patchy or piecemeal. Restorative justice processes should be available everywhere, so that all who want to use them have this choice. It is an approach which deserves a central place in our criminal justice procedures.

Case studies

Claire

Claire, a 38-year-old single mother, and her eight-year-old son Max were victims of an aggravated burglary. The burglar, Sean, broke into their house at night and terrorised them. Sean was caught, convicted and sent to prison for three years. But Max's

nightmares persisted. As the time approached for Sean to be released, Claire grew anxious. She approached her local Citizens' Advice Bureau, which referred her to the local Mediation and Reparation Service. The mediators visited Sean who had just been released. He was surprised and upset to hear that his victims were still frightened. A meeting was arranged at a community centre. Sean apologised in full and reassured Claire he had no intention of burgling her house again. Claire accepted the apology and re-assurance, and found the meeting helpful. Max's nightmares stopped soon afterwards.

Robin

Robin, aged 17, had been in and out of trouble for three years, with offences of theft from a car, theft from shops and four burglaries. He had fallen out with his family because of his offending. The local Intensive Support and Supervision Programme arranged a Family Group Conference using an independent co-ordinator. In the end 15 people attended: Robin, his mother, father and sister; his friend and his parents, and an uncle; his foster mother who had looked after him at one point; his social

worker, a police officer, a Youth Offending Team officer, a Victim Support worker (the victims did not want to come themselves) and a volunteer mentor. Robin took on board the statements made by the Victim Support worker about the effects of burglary on victims, which he had not realised before. The plan formulated by the conference centred round Robin making a home with his friend's family and getting a job. A year later he was still managing to keep out of trouble.

Steve and Gilda

In 1984, Steve Figaroa was an angry, socially excluded teenager of 17. Following a drug deal that went wrong, he killed a young man and his innocent girlfriend Raynell. Steve was caught and convicted of first-degree murder and sentenced to life. After 10 years in prison, he received a letter from Raynell's mother Gilda. She had been working with Texas Victims' Services, trying unsuccessfully to come to terms with her loss. She wrote to Steve at their suggestion, so that some of the questions that were driving her to despair might be answered.

Over a year later, the Rev. David Doerfler of Texas Victims' Services in Austin acted as a go-between, to see if a face-to-face meeting might be appropriate. In the end they met in prison, for a three-hour session. Steve explained the circumstances of the killing. Gilda told him of her feeling of continuing pain. This clearly was a shock to Steve, who had not considered her feelings for 10 years. When Gilda showed him pictures of her daughter, he wept and apologised.

• Roger Graef writes, lectures and broadcasts regularly on crime and media issues. Best known for his award-winning BBC series on the Thames Valley Police, which influenced government policy, he is also the author of *Talking Blues: Police in their own words* and *Living Dangerously: Young Offenders in their own words.*

• The above information is a press release regarding the publication of the book *Why Restorative Justice?*, by Roger Graef published by the Calouste Gulbenkian Foundation, February 2001, £4.99.

Crime: time for real *zero* tolerance

By Simon Heffer

As a visitor to America before the days of zero tolerance policing, I remember being shocked by drive-by shootings and car-jackings, and thanking God that they didn't happen in Britain.

However, this week's murder of an estate agent in a London street by men who wanted his car, and a Yardie shoot-out in broad daylight a few miles away, suggests that Dodge City has arrived in our capital.

It was ironic that these incidents should have happened in the week that Home Secretary David Blunkett entertained New York police chief Bill Bratton, inventor of zero tolerance.

Mr Blunkett, who is keen to cultivate a tough-guy image, was clearly hoping that some of Mr Bratton's robustness might rub off on him, but he remains a veritable pussycat by comparison.

At the root of our violent crime problem are two things: the widespread 'recreational' use of drugs and the politically correct obsession with so-called institutional racism that has prevented the police from dealing with the threat posed by organised gangs of black youths.

These problems, encouraged by the Government, are closely related. Unless they are tackled we will see urban anarchy continue and lead to many more innocent victims.

Almost 80 per cent of crime in our cities is drug-related. It includes either rival gangs killing each other in turf wars, or the rampant theft of goods such as mobile phones or high-performance cars to provide the money either for the next fix or for a larger consignment of drugs to sell.

And, yet, this hypocritical Government continues to support initiatives which tolerate drug use.

A couple of years ago, Ann Widdecombe was howled down for

We must treat causes as well as symptoms; and that means true zero tolerance of all crimes by all criminals

---

suggesting that there was no point in zero tolerance unless it extended to drugs. She was quite right, but it damaged her political career.

If we are serious about tackling crime, we must follow New York's example and get nasty with everyone who does *anything* illegal, and that includes all those 'innocent' young people using drugs 'recreationally' – without whom there would be no drugs trade.

Of course the great majority of black Britons are decent and law-abiding but some impoverished young blacks seem to be responsible for a large proportion of violent, drugs-related crime and gangsterism. Scotland Yard has been well aware of this problem for a long time, but, even before the Macpherson report into the murder of black teenager Stephen Lawrence, officers were nervous of targeting black suspects for fear of the political fall-out.

We must treat causes as well as symptoms; and that means true zero tolerance of all crimes by all criminals – whatever section of the community they are from.

ADDITIONAL RESOURCES

You might like to contact the following organisations for further information. Due to the increasing cost of postage, many organisations cannot respond to enquiries unless they receive a stamped, addressed envelope.

Calouste Gulbenkian Foundation
98 Portland Place
London, W1N 4ET
Tel: 020 7636 5313
Fax: 020 7637 3421
E-mail: info@gulbenkian.org.uk
Web site: www.gulbenkian.org.uk
Charity dealing with social welfare and education issues. Funds research and the publication of reports on their findings. Ask for their publications list.

The Children's Society
Edward Rudolf House
Margery Street
London, WC1X 0JL
Tel: 020 7841 4400
Fax: 020 7841 4500
E-mail: information@the-childrens-society.org.uk
Web site: www.childrenssociety.org.uk
The Children's Society is one of the largest and most innovative children's charities in Britain, founded in 1881 and working through projects all over England. We reach out to nearly 40,000 children and young people every year helping to find solutions to the very serious problems they face.

The Howard League for Penal Reform
1 Ardleigh Road
London, N1 4HS
Tel: 020 7249 7373
Fax: 020 7249 7788
E-mail: howardleague@ukonline.co.uk
Web site: www.howardleague.org
The Howard League works for humane and rational reform of the penal system. They research and comment on criminal justice policy and practice, holding conferences and debates, publishing books and reports.

Metropolitan Police Service
New Scotland Yard
Broadway
London, SW1H 0BG
Tel: 020 7230 1212
Fax: 020 7230 4276
Web site: www.met.police.uk
The Metropolitan Police Service is famed around the world and has a unique place in the history of policing. It is by far the largest of the police forces that operate in Greater London. (The others include the City of London Police, the British Transport Police and the Royal Parks Constabulary.)

Nacro
169 Clapham Road
London, SW9 0PU
Tel: 020 7582 6500
Fax: 020 7735 4666
E-mail: communications@nacro.org.uk
Web site: www.nacro.org.uk
Nacro's vision is a safer society where everyone belongs, human rights are respected and preventing crime means tackling social exclusion and re-integrating those who offend.

The Suzy Lamplugh Trust
14 East Sheen Avenue
London, SW14 8AS
Tel: 020 8392 1839
Fax: 020 8392 1830
E-mail: trust@suzylamplugh.org
Web site: www.suzylamplugh.org
The Suzy Lamplugh Trust is the national charity for personal safety. It aims to create a safer society and enable people to live safer lives, providing practical personal safety advice for everyone, everyday, everywhere.

Youth Justice Board
11 Carteret Street
London, SW1H 9DL
Tel: 020 7271 3033
Fax: 020 7271 3030
Web site: www.youth-justice-board.gov.uk
The Youth Justice Board for England and Wales will help rebuild communities and promote decent opportunities for all by preventing offending by children and young people.

YWCA
Clarendon House
52 Cornmarket Street
Oxford, OX1 3EJ
Tel: 01865 304200
Fax: 01865 204805
E-mail: info@ywca-gb.org.uk
Web site: www.ywca-gb.org.uk
The YWCA in England and Wales is a force for change for women who are facing discrimination and inequalities of all kinds.

INDEX

ACKNOWLEDGEMENTS

The publisher is grateful for permission to reproduce the following material.

While every care has been taken to trace and acknowledge copyright, the publisher tenders its apology for any accidental infringement or where copyright has proved untraceable. The publisher would be pleased to come to a suitable arrangement in any such case with the rightful owner.

Overview

Britain leads the world on risk of being assaulted, © Telegraph Group Limited, London 2002, *Violence rules: not OK*, © Telegraph Group Limited, London 2002, *Notifiable offences recorded by the police*, © Crown Copyright is reproduced with the permission of the Controller of Her Majesty's Stationery Office, *Extent of crime in 2000*, © Crown Copyright is reproduced with the permission of the Controller of Her Majesty's Stationery Office, *Chance of being a crime victim 'at 20-year low'*, © Telegraph Group Limited, London 2002.

Chapter One: Young People and Crime

Youth crime, © Nacro, *Levels of disorder in 2000 BCS*, © Crown Copyright is reproduced with the permission of the Controller of Her Majesty's Stationery Office, *What turns children into criminals?*, © Youth Justice Board, *Young adults*, © The Howard League for Penal Reform, *Statistics on young adults*, © The Howard League for Penal Reform, *Young people's attitudes to crime*, © Youth Justice Board, *More girls than boys go shoplifting*, © Telegraph Group Limited, London 2002, *Bad girls or bad laws?*, © YWCA of Great Britain, *Violent crime by the young*, © Telegraph Group Limited, London 2002, *Huge rise in mobile phone thefts from children*, © Guardian Newspapers Limited 2002, *Young offenders 'denied fresh air'*, © Guardian Newspapers Limited 2002, *Conditions for child prisoners breach international standards*, © The Howard League for Penal Reform, *Time to educate the criminals?*, © Kirstine Hansen, *Missing the grade*, © The Howard League for Penal Reform, *Young offenders' institutions failing to educate inmates*, © Guardian Newspapers Limited 2002, *Offences committed*, © Youth Justice Board, *Youth justice*, © Metropolitan Police, *Woolf's ruling could put more children in jail*, © Telegraph Group Limited, London 2002, *Serious crime by the young doubles in 7 years*, © Telegraph Group Limited, London 2002.

Chapter Two: Crime Prevention

Living safely, © The Suzy Lamplugh Trust, *Tackling street crime*, © Metropolitan Police, *Children and crime reduction*, © The Howard League for Penal Reform, *Young victims count too*, © Guardian Newspapers Limited 2002, *Mobile muggings highlight a wider problem*, © Guardian Newspapers Limited 2002, *Lokit, Mrkit, KEPit, Usit, DntL0sit*, © Metropolitan Police, *Young people and Neighbourhood Watch*, © Crown Copyright is reproduced with the permission of the Controller of Her Majesty's Stationery Office, *Lessons from Europe?*, © The Howard League for Penal Reform, *Age of criminal responsibility*, © The Howard League for Penal Reform, *Why restorative justice?*, © Calouste Gulbenkian Foundation, *Crime: time for real zero tolerance*, © The Daily Mail, February 2002.

Photographs and illustrations:

Pages 1, 15, 19, 32: Bev Aisbett; pages 3, 12, 16, 25, 31, 34: Simon Kneebone; pages 5, 27, 29: Fiona Katauskas; pages 13, 36, 39: Pumpkin House.

Craig Donnellan
Cambridge
April, 2002